Winning The Landlord-Tenant War

Winning The Landlord-Tenant War

A Tenants Guide

Dr. Forest B. Wortham

Writer's Showcase

San Jose New York Lincoln Shanghai

Writer's Showcase
an imprint of iUniverse.com, Inc.

For information address:
iUniverse.com, Inc.
5220 S 16th, Ste. 200
Lincoln, NE 68512
www.iuniverse.com

All information contained herein is subject to change
and variation according to state local and regional rulings.

ISBN: 0-595-17931-2

Printed in the United States of America

DEDICATION

This book is dedicated to my wife Laurie and daughter Nicole who supported me throughout this endeavor. Also to my mother Mary who inspired in me the desire to reach for the sky.

Contents

EDITORIAL METHOD

Chicago Manual of Style 14th Edition
Websters Collegiate Dictionary 10th Edition
Marcy Hall at Island Edits

Introduction

The initial motivation for writing this book was based on my experience as an advocate for tenants/college students at Penn State University that lived in off-campus rental properties in State College, Pennsylvania. Since that time, I have also had the opportunity to work in the property management business—specifically, public housing—for the Fort Myers Housing Authority HUD (Housing and Urban Development) in Fort Myers, Florida, which helped me see things from a landlord's perspective. Consequently, this book is written from the perspective of a tenant advocate and property management employee in two distinctly different environments.

Over the years, students and landlords alike have come to me with what I considered as unbelievable stories, each group complaining they had been wronged. As a result, I determined it was time to compile the various experiences and stories of both groups to help individuals looking to rent on their own for the first time.

As a tenant advocate at Penn State University, I listened to tenant horror stories about losing deposits and moving into units that were unfit for human habitation. I also heard stories about unscrupulous landlords who took security deposits and refused to make needed repairs. Landlords also shared unbelievable stories about tenants structurally redesigning the units without permission and parties that left drunken bodies and body fluids throughout the rental complex.

Similarly, when I worked for the Fort Myers Housing Authority, I listened to management complain about violent, angry, hostile tenants who destroyed property, broke rules, and generally made life miserable for themselves and management. In both situations, I was faced with individuals who were entrenched in their behavior and beliefs. Both groups also believed the other was vehemently wrong and that they were treated unjustly.

The issues facing tenants are the same no matter what their background or where they are living. Young families, singles, college students, public housing residents, and first-time renters on limited incomes all go through the same basic steps to rent a place to live. Everyone signs a lease; they usually have to put down a deposit; they have to pay the rent; and when they leave, they want their security deposit returned.

College towns, where my experience with rental housing began, are similar to most communities in the United States. There are a variety of rental options—single rooms, apartments, houses, condominiums, mobile homes, and town houses. The choice is often broad and varied, just like the prices that accompany the properties.

Finding and renting a place to live is not an experience for the timid. First-time renters are thrown into an arena in which they have no experience. Much of what a first-time renter encounters is magnified by their naiveté. First time renters learn about the perils and pitfalls of renting through trial and error interspersed with family and friends' advice. Even family members who consider themselves well versed in property management and law are often stumped when trying to decipher the rental business in college towns and big-city rental markets. Understanding the rental market and signing a lease are made more frustrating by the magnitude of paperwork that is required, the excitement of finding the place you really want, the unique language of the rental industry, and the fact that anyone can be a landlord without training.

The situation is made worse by the fact that there is no standard lease that all landlords use, nor is there a standardized set of rental rules and regulations within or across states. Likewise, there are no classes targeted toward renters to help them understand tenants' rights and responsibilities.

The result is that renters and their cosigners end up signing leases without understanding the legality of the signed documents until it is too late. These same leases are often found in office supply stores in a standard format, while some landlords make up their own leases—or no lease at all.

If you look for information on renting, what you will find are books written for property managers and landlords, or books focused on specific geographical areas. With all of these obstacles, it's not surprising that renters are ill prepared to deal with renting and the logistics associated with it.

Because the search for rental property is a daunting process, some renters resort to agencies or individuals that charge a fee to find them a place to live. Some renters employ real estate agents to find rental properties, while others enlist agencies or brokers that list available properties. In rent-controlled cities where the rental properties are at a premium, it is not unusual for people to read the obituaries to see who died and where they lived in hopes of renting the assumed now-vacant unit. Waiting lists are also not uncommon in highly desirable areas. In large metropolitan areas and small desirable communities, it is not uncommon to see storefront operations that list rental properties.

Students going away to college living on their own for the first time typically find it a bit easier to find rental housing if their university has the resources to assist them. Some universities assign a professional staff person with the responsibility of advising students that live off-campus or intend to live off-campus. Other universities provide off-campus students with workshops, seminars, orientations, housing fairs, legal assistance, and tenant mediation groups to deal with their concerns.

Universities with associated law schools tend to have law school students who provide legal information. In an attempt to regulate the quality of off-campus housing, some universities require that the local building code officer inspect rental properties that advertise on-campus. There is yet another group of institutions that purchases off-campus properties and rents them out to the students. Considering the liability and the difficulty of monitoring thousands of rental units, most universities do a good job supporting students that live off-campus while still maintaining a healthy relationship in the community.

Whether living in a college town or in a large metropolitan area, renting is a business that begins and ends with money. Market demand for housing influences the availability, quality, and variety of housing. How much or how little one pays for rent does not guarantee the quality of living. In today's competitive rental market, one has to be a savvy consumer. The cost of renting takes a big bite out of the household finances, and if one is looking at paying their rent with the fruits of their labor from a minimum-wage job of $5.15 an hour, they will soon find that is not enough to pay rent and live. This book will arm the first-time or seasoned renter with the tools needed to win the landlord-tenant war anywhere.

In 1995 there were 23.7 million households with incomes below 50 percent of the national median; 10.9 million were owners, and the remaining 12.8 million rented (Andrews 1998). When you couple that with the 11.5 million students every year who enroll in colleges and universities across the United States, we have a significant portion of the population living in rental housing.

WHERE IT ALL BEGAN

To understand this book, you have to understand the locale from where it originated State College, Pennsylvania home of Penn State University. The area is surrounded by farmland, state parks, and mountains. Over forty thousand students attend the university at the main campus; 74 percent (28,000) of those students live off-campus. Of that number, 53 percent (11,872) live within the 4.98 square miles of the borough that surrounds the university.

The location and the size of the town leaves consumers without the resources they often need. In small college towns, the situation is exacerbated by an infrastructure that is often not prepared to deal with challenges that arise in a large rental market. Small towns typically do not attract large outside investors to build competitively priced rental housing, which further limits consumers' choices. In situations where there are few outside investors, consumers become a captive market. This allows landlords and others to lock in pricing and dictate the type and quality of product/housing that will be available—a take-it-or-leave-it business attitude. This same type of mentality is prevalent in some vacation/resort areas where people (e.g., snow-birds) look for temporary seasonal residences for anywhere from one week to seven months.

Renters, often assume they have no choice when looking for a place to rent in a closed market; they take what is available and feel grateful to get a place. This often leads to an "us versus them" attitude between landlord and tenant.

A typical "us versus them" scenario is when a landlord rents a unit that has not been cleaned, maintained, or repaired for sometime (unbeknownst to the landlord). The new tenant interprets the poor condition of the unit as a message that the landlord does not care about the unit or the tenant and assumes that the landlord is out to rip people off. The tenant then responds by neglecting the unit and, in some cases, vandalizing it.

This leads to the tenant being charged for damages, which results in them forfeiting their security deposit. The result is a never-ending, vicious cycle where no one wins. It's important to note that not all land-lords participate in these unethical business practices, nor do all tenants destroy their rental units in retaliation.

The abdication of the tenant's power and control to the landlord leaves the tenant frustrated, angry, and with no sense of control over his or her living conditions. If both parties knew their rights and responsibilities, perhaps the cycle could stop. Likewise, landlords have to remember that no matter how many rental properties they manage or own, they need tenants to keep the units filled to make money.

Tenants that know their rights and responsibilities are less likely to damage and vandalize units that they know they will be held responsible for. The message tenants receive from a clean, well-maintained unit is that the landlord cares about the property and the tenants. A happy tenant in a clean, well-maintained building is more likely to recommend his or her unit to a friend and is also more likely to maintain the unit.

CHAPTER 1

MONEY: HOW MUCH AND WHAT WILL IT BUY WHERE?

Knowing how much money you have to spend on a place to live and what that money will buy sounds simple. Experience has shown me, time and time again, that most people looking for a place to live look not at how much they can afford but for a place that will improve their social status. People look at units with pools, workout rooms, and various other amenities which increases the price of the unit. Tenants often don't consider that a lack of adequate funds to pay the rent can result in embarrassment, disappointment, stress, and, more important, eviction and lawsuits.

When reviewing your finances, deal only with real money. Don't count on money you plan to get or roommates you hope to find to help pay the rent. Get the cash and the roommates up front; then look for a place you can afford. Economists say your monthly rent should not exceed 25 to 30 percent of your monthly income, and that doesn't include your food and utilities. Therefore, whatever your source of income; part-time or full-time job, grants, loans, scholarships or government assistance, keep it simple: Only buy what you can afford.

When looking for a place to rent, a basic economic principle is in operation: The closer you get to the desired location, the more you will pay. When you add in such variables as the size of the unit and amenities—pools, fitness rooms, business centers, covered parking garages, and Internet connections—you can expect to pay in some way for them.

There are two ways to handle the expenses associated with renting. The first, and the easiest, is to look for a place that includes all your utilities in the rent. The second method is to rent a place where you pay for everything separately.

The latter method requires discipline. You must develop a budget and monitor closely your expenses. Convenience and consistency are reasons for people choosing a place with all the expenses included in the monthly rent. It's much easier to write one monthly check and know everything is paid.

If you choose to rent a place with everything included, remember that you are paying for things like central heating or cooling during the months you are least likely to need them. When the heat is included in the rent in northern climates, there is a good chance the landlord will control when it is turned on and how much comes out. That can be frustrating up North if it gets cold before the heating season begins or stays cold when the season is over.

Landlords who rigidly control the heat are often responding to the behavior of previous tenants that abused the heat-included option by turning the heat up to sauna level and opening the windows in January. With the increasing cost of energy landlords might be less likely to offer an all inclusive rent. Similarly, if you are in any of the southern or western states and air-conditioning is included in the rent, running the cooling system cold enough to cool a side of beef while the window is open is a waste of energy and only causes the landlord to raise your rent—or the next tenant's rent in response to *your* abuse.

If you rent a unit that does not have some or all of the expenses included in the rent, you should expect to spend no less than $250 a month or more for services such as heating, cooling, electrical, water, and trash. Of course, that amount can go up or down depending on the section of the country you live in and the size of the unit. You should also budget for the telephone (local and long distance), cable, renter's insurance, car insurance, transportation, parking, laundry, food, furniture, and entertainment.

In the appendix (see Appendix E) of this book, you will find a chart where you can outline your expenses relative to what you have to spend. When you have determined how much money you have to spend and you know the type of rental unit you want, proceed to the next step.

CHAPTER 2

RENTAL APPLICATIONS, LEASES, AND CLAUSES

APPLICATIONS

Before allowing you to sign a lease, most rental companies need to find out if you can pay for what you want to rent. Landlords accomplish this by having the tenant complete a rental application.

An individual's finances are the only criteria a landlord can use to determine if they qualify to rent an apartment. Due to housing antidiscrimination laws, anything having to due with your ethnic background, race, religion, marital status, gender, or age cannot be used to accept or reject you as a tenant. Smart landlords follow these rules to a tee. A landlord can ask you to provide a referral from the last place you lived therefore, if you were an unfavorable tenant, your acceptance or rejection as a rental applicant could be affected.

Use of rental applications is normal business in the rental industry. How the rental application is used is another story. Most rental companies/landlords require potential tenants to complete a rental application and submit an application fee in order to be considered for a rental unit. The rental application fee is any nonrefundable amount of money an applicant has to pay a landlord at the time of filling out an application. The fee can range from as little as $50 to the equivalent of one month's rent. It depends on the region and the rental company.

This money is used to cover the cost of investigating an applicant's credit worthiness and to hold the unit for the applicant. In some towns, payment of the application fee and submission of the application can lock the tenant into the lease once it is submitted.

Application approval process. In some cities and boroughs, approval of the rental application binds the person applying for the apartment to the lease, making the application fee nonrefundable. Approval of the rental application weighs heavily on the credit check, which verifies the tenant's track record for paying their bills and rent in a timely fashion. Most young people and those that have been out of the workforce don't have much of a credit history. College students and first-time renters often don't have a credit history, or their income level is not adequate.

Landlords work around this cash-flow problem by requiring tenants, with poor credit or no credit history, to obtain a cosigner if they have a low source of income. The cosigner, according to a local landlord in State College PA, can be anyone that is willing to sign the lease guaranteeing that the rent will be paid if the tenant does not pay. Independent young adults whose parents are not contributing to their finances find this approval process demeaning because it often requires that they get a parent, guardian, or friend to co-sign the lease for them. Landlords, however, need to have a definite, secure source of income for the rent.

Rejected applications. After poor credit, the most common reason for rejecting a rental application is an inability to get a cosigner. Rejection, however, does not get one off the financial hook. In State College, Pennsylvania, tenants described how their applications were rejected, yet the landlord told them they were still financially liable for the lease until the unit was rented. Ironically, they were not allowed to live in the unit while they paid. The landlord's rationale often was that the tenant's expressed interest had resulted in the unit being taken off the market while the credit check occurred. Landlords also referred to the binding clauses in the applications that stated very clearly the tenant's responsibility to pay the rent.

Requiring a cosigner is good business sense when people have no visible means of support. What doesn't make sense is to reject someone and not let them move in but require that they pay the rent. Upon talking to attorneys about this practice, I was informed that if a lease is not signed, the application is not binding. The obvious solution to this problem is for individuals not to fill out any applications until they are certain they have identified the unit they want to rent, no matter what town they live in. More important, always read carefully the documents you sign.

LEASES

Leases can be very intimidating, and the process of signing one often lends itself to people just signing their names without reading what they have signed. There are, however, some basic elements a lease needs to have.

It needs to be on paper (duh). It also needs to have the name of the landlord, preferably the location you will be renting, and the price you agreed upon. The date when the lease begins and ends should also be noted.

According to information provided by the Rental Housing On Line Web site, the lease governs the landlord-tenant relationship. It transfers possession, use, and enjoyment of the property from the landlord to the tenant for a specific period of time and for a stated amount of rent. To be enforceable, the rental agreement should satisfy a few basic formalities that help to protect both the landlord and the tenant from fraud or misunderstanding in the event of disagreements or disputes. They are as follows:

- The agreement should be in writing. Most states have adopted a legal doctrine called the Statute of Frauds, which states that contracts for real estate that cannot be performed within one year must be in writing in order to be enforceable. To comply with this statute, leases of one year or more must be written.
- As a practical matter, all leases of any duration should be in writing because the written document provides a record of the terms of the landlord-tenant relationship. A lease is, in fact, a lien on a property, so its terms and conditions should be easily and clearly discernable by the parties, their heirs, or assignees.
- The agreement should be signed and dated. Both the landlord (manager or rental agent) and the tenant or their representative should sign and date the agreement.
- A copy of the agreement should be given to the tenant. All parties to any agreement should be provided with a signed and dated copy to comply with legal requirements and for future reference. The landlord copy should be filed with any other data or documents that pertain to the tenant, and it should be kept at least three years beyond the tenancy.

Most contracts/leases are written so the average person cannot read them. Some states have made it mandatory that contracts/leases be in plain language. In June 1994, Pennsylvania passed a law that required all contracts/leases in the state to be written in plain language—in other words, no legalese. No matter where you live, if your lease is unintelligible, you need to find someone to help you translate the document.

If you live in a state that requires plain-language contracts and yours is not, you need to ask the landlord for a readable document. Check with your state attorney general's office to determine the rules and regulations regarding consumer contracts. No matter how it is written, a lease is a legal binding document; once you sign it, you are bound to it until it terminates. In towns where college students are the primary consumers, you are more likely to find leases that are worded differently than in other areas of the state. Residential leases typically fall into two categories: joint and several, or individual.

Joint and several lease. Joint and several leases are used everywhere. They are beneficial for the landlord in that they hold everyone responsible for the rent. In areas where several related or unrelated individuals share living quarters, this is the more popular type of lease.

Under the joint and several lease in some communities when two or more people related or unrelated live in the same unit, they are responsible for each other's behavior and debts as they relate to the unit. Most landlords using joint and several leases require that only one check be submitted for the complete amount of the rent. The tenants are responsible for collecting the rent from the roommates. Roommates who often don't know each other have to decide whom they can trust to collect the rent.

The question that comes to mind is, why would tenants be living together if they didn't know each other? The answer is that some landlords rent bed spaces, which results in several unrelated people residing in the same unit. In some rental communities with high demand for housing, and inexperienced renters it is not uncommon to have five or six tenants sharing a two-bedroom apartment on a joint and several lease. Tenants should be careful whom they choose to collect the rent. It is not unusual to hear of situations where the person assigned to collect the rent never gave it to the landlord but, of course, the landlord still expected the money.

If one of the roommates does not have his or her portion of the rent at the end of the month, it's the responsibility of the other roommates to pay the difference and coerce the rent out of their noncontributing roommate. If the roommates are unable to pay the rent in full, the landlord has the right to sue all the tenants in the unit (and the parental guarantor) for the total amount of the remaining rent on the lease.

In a joint and several lease, this is referred to as an acceleration clause. The clause allows the landlord to demand that all the remaining rent be rendered in court. Judgments against tenants and their cosigners can, and do, hold up in court. If tenants and their cosigners decide not to appear in court, the landlord can win by default, and cosigners can find a lien on their property if they don't respond to the suit or if they are unable to pay the judgment.

Likewise, if you leave your landlord with an outstanding debt and he or she files suit against you in court and wins, the judgment will go on your credit record, which can affect your getting a job and/or making any major purchases, such as a house or car.

In response to comments about the joint and several lease, the local district justice in State College, Pennsylvania, stated that the "joint and several lease punishes the good tenants that remain in the unit and continue to pay the rent"(Yorks 1991). The tenant that is behind in their rent, however, usually gets away. Under a joint and several lease, roommates end up being financially responsible for each other's behavior in the rental unit. If a roommate damages his or her room, the other tenants could theoretically be charged for the damages unless they let the landlord know.

A tenant once told me of a situation where upon contacting the landlord about a drunken roommate who had damaged the unit, the landlord's position was that landlords do not resolve or mediate roommate problems. Under a joint and several lease, roommates are their "brother and sister's keeper." The only good thing about this type of lease is that it binds everyone to each other.

Again, the responsibility falls on the renter to make conscious decisions when looking for a place to live. Whether short-term or long-term, joint and several leases are designed so the landlord does not have to listen to "Well, my roommate broke the door, but he left last semester, so why should I have to pay?"

Individual lease. Over ten years ago, individual leases were introduced to the off-campus community surrounding Penn State University. In a closed market where joint and several lease had dominated, the students' response was overwhelmingly positive. Many of the landlords in the town saw this as the downfall of the rental empire and thought that they would never be able to collect rent from the tenants.

The marketing strategy for the individual lease was "one bedroom, one person, one lease." Tenants are assigned their own lease, and their liability is limited to the room they occupy and the shared living spaces (i.e., bathroom, living room, dining room, and kitchen). Each tenant is responsible for taking his or her portion of the rent to the landlord. If one tenant defaults on the rent, he or she is dealt with individually. The individual lease has been around for a long time; however, its use in some college towns is limited at best.

Counterfeit individual lease. In some locales where the market has driven landlords to respond to consumer demand for individual leases landlords and property owners offer a counterfeit individual lease. The counterfeit individual lease looks and sounds like the genuine article until you walk into the rental unit. Landlords offering these leases put the same four to six people in a two-bedroom apartment and give them all individual leases.

Theoretically, this sounds good for the tenants. Practically, however, this is not a true individual lease. The counterfeit individual lease, just like the other leases, maintains the right to fill vacant spaces in the rental unit if a tenant leaves the unit and the tenant is still sharing a room.

Like the joint and several lease, in the counterfeit individual lease situation there is no way that individual tenants can be responsible for their own living space if they are sharing their sleeping space with two to three other roommates. There is no separate bedroom/privacy. Living like this is similar to having two or three siblings with no adults or parents to mediate misunderstandings that might occur.

It's important to choose the type of lease you sign as carefully as you choose where you will live. Choose the one that best fits your lifestyle and budget. If you don't like the lease or application and you haven't signed it, attempt to negotiate with the landlord. If he or she refuses to compromise, walk out and find another place to live. It's your money; ask for a lease that meets your needs.

Basic lease components. The following are some of the most common items used in a residential lease according to Rental Housing On Line:

- Identity of the parties to the lease: the landlord or agent, and the tenants (usually defined as those persons who will actually be paying the rent).
- Address of the property and the unit.
- Length of the rental period, and any change in lease conditions in the event of tenant holdover.
- The date on which the tenant will receive the right to use the property.
- Rental amount. A fixed-term tenancy may have to show the total rent due for the term of the lease, as well as the monthly rent payment, in order to be enforceable as to length.
- Late charges provide an incentive to pay the rent on time. However, some state laws (e.g., Massachusetts) limit or even prohibit late charges on residential rent. Others (e.g., Michigan) require the charges to be reasonable. Where state law does not address the issue, courts have. In *Wadsworth v. Starcher*, the Court of Appeals of Ohio ruled that determining whether a late fee is reasonable is totally within a court's discretion. The court held that $5 per day was "unconscionable."
- Security deposits are perhaps the most contentious condition in a landlord-tenant relationship. Consequently, state local laws

addressing security deposits are generally strict and must be considered and addressed in any rental agreement. Most states regulate the amount that can be charged and when and how the deposit will be returned; require that deposits be kept in a separate account; and some require that interest be paid to the tenant. You must check your state law to be sure.

- Occupancy addresses how many adults are allowed to reside in the premises. Some leases limit occupancy to a specific number based on square feet per person. Others use the number of bedrooms as a reasonable limit on occupancy.

- Most leases also prohibit pets entirely or require additional deposits and rent.

- Use and enjoyment is often dictated by the local zoning ordinance, which is likely to permit residential use only and should be so stated.

- Most leases also include language that the premises may not to be used for any illegal purposes.

- The paragraph might also refer to a list of rules often included as an attachment. This might include whether or not assigning and subletting addresses is permitted or prohibited and if written consent is required.

- Upkeep of the premises defines responsibility. Usually, the landlord agrees to repair, while the tenant agrees to maintain.

- The paragraph should also require that all requests for repairs or maintenance be in writing.

- Utilities should be described, assigned, and/or transferred to the tenant's name. The lease should state what utilities are available, those that the tenant is responsible for paying or having in his or her own name, and whether the tenant is responsible for sharing in the cost of utilities for the common areas.

- Other rights and responsibilities of the landlord or tenant not contained in the standard lease provisions but unique to the demised premises should also be included in the written agreement.

- Additional conditions and modifications might address handicap accessibility, swimming pools, pets, waterbeds, laundry equipment, window air conditioners, parking, and any unusual provisions or property conditions.

CLAUSES

Listed below are several clauses from leases that I reviewed while at Penn State. You might find some of them amusing, yet you might find some or all of them in your lease.

- If there is damage in the common area of an apartment building and none of the tenants admit to the damage, all tenants on the floor where the damage occurred will be assessed a charge to cover repairs.
- Tenant agrees to keep the premises clean, and if the landlord determines the unit is unclean, the landlord can call in the health inspector and/or a cleaning service.
- At checkout, the tenant agrees to leave the unit in white-glove condition.
- Tenant has to pay the rent in a lump sum, one money order, one check, or one pile of cash.
- Cash payment is accepted only at the convenience of the landlord.
- If you don't pay your rent because you can't find the landlord to give him or her the cash, the tenant has to pay late fees.
- Tenants are not allowed on the roof at any time. If the tenant is on the roof, he or she agrees to pay $50 each time he or she is warned to get off the roof. The warning will come every five minutes.
- No pets are allowed in the unit, and they cannot come to visit. The tenant agrees to pay $50 if an animal or its bowls, food, or litter is

found on the premises. The tenant will be warned every five minutes if there is an animal in the unit.
- The tenant agrees to pay the landlord $25 every time the landlord has to come and close the windows to the unit if it is raining and there is no one in the unit.
- Tenant agrees to vacuum the unit's carpeting at least once a week.
- Tenants are not allowed to wrestle, fight, practice ballet, do aerobics, or exercise in the unit.
- Tenant agrees to dress appropriately when walking around the rental unit.

The clauses outlined above are the result of interactions landlords have had with previous tenants. It's understandable how a landlord/property owner who has had negative experiences with tenants would include some of these clauses in the lease.

Unlawful lease provisions. The following are some common examples of unlawful lease provisions according to Rental Housing On Line:

- Provisions that are contrary to federal antidiscrimination laws. The lease cannot contain provisions that violate fair housing laws or the Americans with Disabilities Act. For example, it is illegal to include a lease provision that prohibits subleasing to members of minority groups or a provision that charges a higher security deposit to a disabled tenant or to a family with children.
- Eviction of the tenant without due process. The tenant cannot be evicted from the unit without notice or a hearing on the issue.
- Similarly, leases (in almost every state) can no longer contain a provision that permits a landlord to take possession of the tenant's personal property (landlord liens) without due process because of nonpayment of rent.
- Waiver of habitability by the tenant. The lease cannot contain a provision in which the tenant agrees to waive the landlord's

warranty of habitability or hold the landlord harmless for breaches of the warranty.

- The "as-is" clause that is commonly found in most lease agreements is not a valid lease clause in most states. In every state but three, a landlord is required to keep residential premises habitable.
- Additionally, the landlord can be held responsible for injuries that result from the condition of a rental property, regardless of a habitability lease provision or the tenant agreeing to correct the problem.
- Typically, the term *habitable* includes major systems, such as roof, plumbing, heating, air permeation, conditioning, structural elements, or any unsafe condition. Carpet, paint, and other cosmetic items generally do not affect the habitability of the home unless they present a health hazard.
- However, landlords have discovered to their dismay that every judge seems to have his or her own definition of *habitable*. One judge recently determined that a kitchen was not habitable because the stove did not work and reduced the rent for the house by 25 percent for the period it did not work. In another case, rent was abated for a month because a loose carpet bar was a tripping hazard.
- Waiver of the landlord's legal responsibilities. Provisions that waive the landlord's legal responsibilities are void. For example: a provision that prohibits the tenant from holding the landlord responsible for the landlord's negligent acts, or a provision that attempts to circumvent landlord-tenant law.
- Provisions that penalize the tenant for complying with the law. The lease cannot contain a provision that penalizes the tenant for informing government authorities of any landlord violation of the law.
- For instance, a lease provision that calls for immediate eviction if the tenant informed the building or health authorities of an unsafe condition on the premises is not permitted. In fact, most

state law now addresses so-called retaliatory eviction and pro-hibits eviction for any cause immediately following a complaint to authorities.

Right of entry clause. The right of entry clause is an innocuous clause that few people notice until the landlord or his or her representative enters the unit unannounced. Right of entry allows the landlord to enter the premises anytime to make repairs or show the unit. The prob-lem with this clause is that maintenance men also think that they can enter the unit without notice at any time.

According to Rental Housing On Line, amateur landlords often think that because they are the owners, they may go into a rental property anytime they wish. That is not true. Under the law, a tenant has a right to "quiet enjoyment."

A major point of contention over tenants' right to privacy in recent years results from onerous new rental-property-only inspection ordi-nances being adopted by various municipalities across the country. In many cases, the local rental inspection laws do not acknowledge the tenant's right to deny access to anyone, even city rental inspectors, "without probable cause to believe that a crime has been committed" as is required under the Forth Amendment to the U.S. Constitution. The same local officials are quick to acknowledge that they are prohibited from entering an owner-occupied residence without permission or a warrant.

My suggestion is that before signing the lease, strike the right of entry clause and have the landlord initial it. Then put in a clause that reads the landlord can enter the premises only after giving the tenant a twenty-four-hour notice, or some other reasonable time, unless it's an emergency. According to the Oklahoma State University Renters Advisory Council, in order to remove an undesirable clause from a lease, the relevant words must be crossed out. The tenant and the landlord (or the landlord's authorized agent) must then put their initials next to the corrections. This must be done on both the landlord's copy and the tenant's copy for the changes to be fully enforceable.

Put this clause in to eliminate landlords and their representatives from walking in on you unannounced at any time. If you have no other alternative but to accept the lease with the clauses, at least put it in writing to the landlord that you are not in agreement with the clauses as outlined in the lease. Remember that if the landlord or his or her representative walks in your unit, you still do not have the right to change the lock without letting him or her know. If you do change the lock, you must get permission and give the landlord a copy of the key.

According to the Oklahoma State University Renters Advisory Council, it is crucial for the tenant to read the entire lease and to look for areas where problems could arise:

- Does the lease include, in writing, all the promises your landlord has made to you?
- Does the lease ask you to agree that landlord is not liable for repairs?
- Who pays the landlord's attorney fees if you go to court?
- Does the lease ask you to waive the right to a jury trial?
- Does the lease ask you to agree to obey rules that the landlord might not have even made yet?
- Does the lease ask you to agree to pay possible extra rent, assessments, property taxes, et cetera, that can be assessed upon your landlord?
- Does the lease give the landlord free reign to enter the apartment at any time?
- Who is liable if you or your personal property is injured or damaged?
- Does the lease ask you to agree that no one else will live in the rented property unless they are named in the lease?
- Do improvements you build belong to the landlord?
- Does the lease ask you to state that premises are fine and to accept them as they are?

CHAPTER 3

WHAT YOU SEE IS WHAT YOU GET

THE RENTAL AGENT LOOKING AT THE UNIT

Now it's time for you to make an appointment to meet the rental agent at his or her office. This is the individual whom you will be doing business with for the next year or more. Before you walk into the rental office, remember that the job of the rental agent is to keep the building at 100 percent occupancy. In other words, once you get past the baked cookies and dressed-to-kill look, remember that this is a business deal and the purpose is to make the sale if you qualify to live in the unit.

When you walk into the office, make note of how the employees treat you and the other customers. If they are abrupt and react as though you are an intrusion in their day, make a note. No matter how crowded or busy the office, this is a good indicator of how you will be treated as a tenant. It usually doesn't get any better.

The rental agent shouldn't be deciding on the spot whether you can afford to rent the unit or whether you fit in the community. The credit check will take care of that. Rental agents should also not discriminate based on race, age, gender, religion, or ethnic background. If you believe you have been denied the opportunity to apply for a rental unit or that you were rebuffed because you fit any of the categories listed above, contact your fair housing office.

Beware of anyone who tries to pressure you into signing a lease on the spot. Even if you know that housing is limited and this might be your best deal, you need to let the individual know you are a customer and you expect to be treated as such. Beware of the statement "I have several other people looking at the unit after you. If you want to hold it, give me a deposit." Don't allow yourself to be pressured into a hasty decision.

Watch out for lowballing. That's when the rent advertised is extremely low; however, when you arrive to look at the unit, there are none available at the advertised price—or the one that is available is unlivable. Upon seeing your disappointment, the landlord shows you a higher-priced unit that is in better condition.

This type of behavior should be reported to the state attorney general's office of consumer affairs and/or the Better Business Bureau. In areas where there are a lot rental properties, competition will drive some property owners to offer perks, such as one free month's rent, a free microwave, mountain bikes. As good as these free things sound, don't let these goodies confuse you in your search for a place to live.

TALK IS CHEAP

The price on the signed lease is the price you are obligated to pay. The price should not go up because the landlord made a mistake and put the wrong price in. This is a business deal; therefore, get everything in writing. Once the lease is signed, it's your word against the landlord's. The landlord is in the business of filling units to make a profit. Get the names of everyone you talk to. Ask how long they have been in the business of property management.

In high-density rental areas, property owners/mangers will often hire temporary workers during heavy rental periods to staff their offices. These hard-working, well-meaning individuals sometimes unknowingly give out incorrect information. It's important to remember that throughout the rental process, you are the customer, and it's your money. The amount quoted per month adds up to thousands of dollars over a period of nine or twelve months.

What Does It Look Like?

Good customer-service-oriented rental companies will show you the unit that is available to rent. Other companies, however, will keep a model unit available for showing. Model apartments rarely look like the place you will live in, other than the layout. Few of them have been occupied for extended periods and, therefore, show very little tenant occupancy wear. If you rent a place without seeing it, you are playing rental roulette. You really don't know what you are getting. Once you see the unit, have the landlord write the number of the unit on the lease before it is signed.

If the landlord refuses to show you the actual unit, think twice about renting from the company. Remember earlier when I talked about *right of entry*? That's where the rule should operate to your benefit when looking at an occupied apartment. This could be an indication of their level of customer service. If all else fails, find out what building or floor the rental unit is on. Knock on a few doors; ask the residents what they think about living there. What is the management and maintenance like and, of course, what's the building like in terms of security and noise?

Before you leave, walk around the property. Is the lawn manicured? Is there trash blowing about? Do the windows of the units have screens? Are there broken windows? What does the entrance to the building look like? Are there fingerprints on the doors? Does the front door welcome you, or does it make you want to walk away? What about the parking lot? Is it well lit and well paved with no potholes?

All of these things send a message about management's attitude about the property and its tenants. That attitude could be reflected later in your relationship with the landlord. To gain an even better perspective, visit the property after-hours and on the weekend. Go by the trash dumpster. Is it filled overflowing? Do they recycle? Sunday evening or early Monday morning gives you an idea as to management's concern about the image of the unit.

Questions a tenant might ask. According to *Landlord-Rights and Responsibilities (1993),* before agreeing to rent, the tenant should ask the following questions:

- How much is the rent?
- When is the rent due?
- To whom and where should the rent be paid?
- Is a security deposit required?
- To whom should problems and repairs be referred?
- Will there be an oral or written lease?
- Will there be late fees?
- Must the rent be in special form; i.e. one check only, cash is acceptable, etc.
- Will the tenant be renting for a month-to-month or a year-to-year term?
- Is there an application fee? How much is it and is it refundable?
- If the application is approved will the tenant be committed to sign the lease?

CHAPTER 4

SECURITY OUTSIDE AND INSIDE

SECURITY OUTSIDE

Building security is something everyone should be aware of; however, most people ignore it until something unfortunate happens. The ideal apartment building has a secure locking system on all entrances and exits—which are also well lit—and security personnel and observant neighbors to keep intruders out. If the building has an intercom system that visitors use to call tenants, that's an additional measure of security that allows you to screen guests.

Some of the more modern buildings have an in-house cable broadcast system where you can view who is buzzing you over a closed circuit in house television channel. Buildings with elevators should have an emergency call system in the elevators and the garages. Some of the newer buildings that are being built have security systems wired into the management's office, which have to be armed and disarmed upon entry and exit.

As you walk around the building to assess the security, look to see if there are people loitering near the building. The best time to assess this is during the evening hours and weekend. What's the parking like? Is it on the street or in a garage?

Street parking is great until you come home late one evening and you have to park five blocks away. It is also a bear if it snows and you get plowed in or if you caught in the middle of a torrential summer downpour. Not to mention the fact that when a major snowstorm occurs in most northern states, you have to get your vehicle off the road or it will be towed and ticketed. Likewise, in a torrential downpour in Florida, it is not unusual for the water to come down so fast that you have two to three feet of water in the parking lot that you have to wade through to get to your unit.

If you park in a lot or a garage, is it well lit? Is the parking assigned by unit, or is it just open? Do they have security people that patrol the area?

COMMON SENSE SECURITY STEPS THE TENANT CAN TAKE

In small rural towns and college communities tenants tend to let their guards down. No mater where you rent, it's important to remain vigilant when it comes to safety and security. Smallness does not guarantee the area is crime free.

Tom King, the chief of police in State College, Pennsylvania, stated in a meeting that, "Students residing in State College are often the victims of crimes of opportunity" (1994). What this means is that college students often put themselves in situations where they are vulnerable targets for opportunistic criminals. College students however are no different than any other group of renters. While working at a Housing Urban Development property in southwest Florida it was not unusual for me to see the residents exhibit the same carelessness in regards to security that I had seen on college campuses. Listed below are several examples of crimes of opportunity:

- Leaving the unit unlocked to eliminate carrying keys
- Coming home drunk and not locking the door
- Playing the music on their new stereo loud enough to be heard by potential thieves
- Walking home alone and drunk
- Keeping large amounts of cash or jewelry visible in the living unit for friends and guests to readily see
- Answering machine messages that announce they are not at home
- Leaving windows or sliding doors open when they aren't at home or when they are sleeping
- Tenants that leave notes on their door indicating they are not at home and when they expect to return

These are just some of the more blatant examples of how tenants place themselves in danger. In most towns, it's not only what you do; it's where you do it. Some apartment buildings and houses are known for their parties. These places tend to have increased traffic around the entrances and exits on the weekends. When party crashers can't get in by following someone in, they ring every bell in the building until they get someone to respond. This usually occurs around 2 A.M.—when the bars let out. If, out of frustration or annoyance, you buzz someone in, you could be letting a potential thief—or worse—in your building. Likewise tenants who allow non residents to hangout and cause damage where they live and not report the interlopers encourage an unsafe living environment.

Security Inside the Unit

Examine the construction of the door and the windows. Are the outside doors solid, or do they have a hollow core? Hollow-core doors can be broken into with a well-placed kick or fist. On the other hand, solid-core doors are more difficult to break or damage. Look at the doorjamb; is it structurally sound, or does it look tampered with?

Does the door have a dead-bolt lock or a spring-loaded lock? Spring-loaded locks have a button on the inside in the doorknob that you push to lock, and they are extremely ineffective against burglars. On the other hand, dead-bolt locks are designed to withstand the attempts of burglars with their half-inch to one-inch bolts.

Tourist areas, college towns, and beach towns, tend to draw a transient population with new residents moving in and out of units several times a year. Consequently, there are lots of keys to units being transferred, turned in, copied, and lost through the year. In some towns, there is no guarantee that the locks on the doors have been rekeyed. Consequently, there is no telling how many copies of the keys to your unit are floating around out there.

Confirm with the landlord that there are no copies of the key floating around with previous tenants. If the landlord cannot verify that all the keys have been turned in, ask them to rekey the unit at their expense before you move in and sign the lease. If they are unwilling to cover the cost, ask if you can get a locksmith to change the lock or the core, and then give the landlord a copy of the new key.

If your outside door doesn't have a peephole, ask the landlord to install one. This will allow you to look out and see who's at the door without opening it. Check your windows; are the locks adequate? Can you secure the windows to let air in and out without allowing intruders in? There are special units you can install on the windows that will allow you to do that.

If you have a sliding glass door, get a sturdy two-by-four, and put it between the door and the end of the wall. This will prevent the door from being opened if you are not there. You can also have the two-by-four cut slightly shorter to allow air in, but not wide enough to let a person get through. If the landlord balks at any of these suggested security measures, you need to document his or her refusal to change or upgrade the security.

Send him or her a letter stating that he or she will be held responsible if anything happens.

You have put the landlord on notice about a potential problem. If you are handy with tools and you want that extra measure of security, install a burglar arm in your unit. Most home-builder stores have security systems that can be installed by an amateur. Some of them can even be installed with a module that calls the police when and if someone breaks in.

SECURITY RESOURCES

Call the local police station and ask which neighborhood has the most police activity. Ask them whether the neighborhood you are considering is safe, as well as which neighborhoods you should avoid. Get recommendations from individuals in authority, friends, and community residents as to which areas they consider safe. At the Microsoft Network Web site, visitors can retrieve brief outlines of security, demographics, and education in various neighborhoods in the United States.

CHAPTER 5

ROOMMATES: CAN'T LIVE WITH THEM, CAN'T LIVE WITHOUT THEM

In an era of television shows such as *Friends*, *Felicity*, and *Two Guys and a Girl*, the implied message to the general population is that living with multiple roommates is sexy, economical, fun, and conflict free. According to the media, these living accommodations also come with the opportunity to cohabitate with the roomies. Despite the media aura of living with friends, economics is probably the driving force for people who seek out roommates.

The property rental section of any local newspaper is a good barometer of the cost to rent in the selected community. Where the rental market is competitive, renters will find property owners giving a month's free rent, microwaves, and even in some cases a finder's fee when tenants refer a new tenant that signs a lease. Where that market is not competitive, landlords can and do adopt a take-it-or-leave-it attitude.

In some towns, rents are advertised on a low per-person rate to get the customer in the door. Seldom is there mention of the total cost of the unit in the advertising. Consequently, a typical two-bedroom unit that would house two tenants is rented to five or six tenants, and one-bedroom units rent to as many as three tenants. These shared living conditions are conducive to roommate conflict, vandalism, violence, noise, and worn-out rental units. Tenants also take it upon themselves to invite their friends to live with them to help defray living expenses by sharing the rent. Most of the time this happens without the approval of the landlord, which is grounds for eviction.

Many of today's young tenants come from homes where they did not have to share a room—if they did, it was with one person, not multiple siblings. Most tenants, therefore, want their own private bedroom. From a university perspective, sharing a residence hall room (dorm) with another person is part of growing and developing as a young person in college. To help people living on-campus, however, there are trained and educated professionals that can help mediate conflicts when they occur.

On the other hand, sharing a two-bedroom apartment off-campus with five or six roommates is an invitation to disaster. When you add in the fact that landlords are not required to help mediate roommate conflicts in these overcrowded conditions, you have a volatile mixture. Once you move into your own rental unit with a group of individuals, you and your roommates are responsible for resolving your own problems.

There is no legal precedent or obligation that requires a landlord to change your roommate or apartment or to cancel your lease when you have a roommate conflict. When there is a concession to this hard and fast rule, it is usually at the discretion of the landlord. Consequently, when apartment or room switches occur, it's usually the tenant that has to find a person to take over their lease—or else face the prospect of paying for two leases.

The more traditional response to roommate conflicts is that the individual who is uncomfortable moves out, leaving the remaining roommates with one less roommate and a lot more space, along with a bill. If you choose to live in a situation with three or more people sharing a bedroom, choose your roommates carefully, and establish rules and regulations early in the relationship.

Finding a Roommate

How and where you identify roommates is extremely important to avoid the "roommate from hell." Tenants use a variety of methods to identify roommates. Some people post adds at work, in the grocery store, and even in the newspaper. At colleges, people put signs on bulletin boards around campus. If you use this open-advertising method, you need to extensively screen potential roommates to see if you are compatible.

Some landlords attempt to help tenants find roommates. I have seen some of them use complex computer-matching services, while others use informal pizza parties. On the other hand, some landlords only go so far as to separate smokers from nonsmokers. No matter which method is used, you cannot afford to sit back and let someone or something match you up without asking some basic questions of your potential roommate. Nothing replaces your own personal interaction and judgment. No matter how you find a roommate, you must establish a line of communication before the individual walks through the door. You have to work with the individual, and they have to work with you to make the relationship successful.

Finding a compatible roommate is not a simple process. In identifying roommates, be very careful who you agree to let live with you. Over the years, tenants have come to me with horror stories about their roommates. A young woman told of a male roommate being assigned to her apartment who had just been released from prison. While another group of young ladies told of how their roommate sublet her space in a two bedroom apartment to a male who was to share the bedroom. Individuals intending to live together should start by examining their own personal likes and dislikes. You have to know yourself before talking to a potential roommate. Once you have determined your own likes and dislikes, it's easier seeing how you and your potential roommate are similar and dissimilar.

To start the process, use the roommate questionnaire (see Appendix H). The roommate questionnaire is a list of basic questions that potential roomies can use to initiate discussion about personal values, such as taste in music, smoking, parties, and overnight guests. The roommate agreement (see Appendix I) also outlines financial and housekeeping obligations. Once the roommate agreement is completed, both roommates should write in their permanent home address, telephone number, and driver's license, and sign and notarize the document. This way you are both covered in case either one of you decides to walk out of the deal or the other has to sue. Check with an attorney or legal aid to determine the legality of this agreement in your state.

A final word of caution in your quest to find a roommate: Be extremely careful about living with people whom you consider to be your best friends and have known all your life. The person who is your best buddy or whom you work with in the same department on daily basis might not be your best choice for a roommate. Living with this type of person gives you the opportunity to learn his or her faults and he or she to learn yours. It is probably the best way to ruin a friendship.

ROOMMATE CONFLICTS

Whether you decide to live with your best high school buddy, a casual friend, or complete stranger, conflict eventually occurs. How you resolve conflicts will determine how you get along for the remainder of the lease. A few simple questions can avoid problems down the road. The easiest way to deal with roommate conflict is to talk about it. If you are discussing a problem, whether you are arguing about it or talking civilly, you are at least communicating.

Roommates who don't talk about problems and expect them to disappear usually end up blowing up in each other's face. Hence, it is safe to say that if you decide to room with your best friend from high school because you have always gotten along, you are not guaranteed a conflict-free environment. In fact, when roommates are best friends, they are less likely to be honest in their communication for fear of hurting each other's feelings.

Roommate conflicts often focus on what I will term as *housekeeping issues*, such as overnight guests, cleaning, cooking, and use of alcohol. These are just some of the issues you might have to deal with. If you can clarify these issues early in the game, you have a better chance of surviving the year. A roommate is an individual who shares your living space with you. You don't have to be bosom buddies, nor do you have to do everything together. In fact, it's likely that the more you are away from each other, the better chance you have at getting along with each other when you are together in the unit.

An additional factor one needs to consider when choosing a roommate is the number of roommates residing in the unit. Informal student feedback indicates that roommate relations are more positive when there is an even number of roommates versus an odd number. There is less likelihood of being left out of things or being ostracized with an even number of roommates to pair up.

GUESTS/VISITORS

Benjamin Franklin once said, "fish and visitors smell in three days." In other words house guests should not visit for more than three days. When living with roommates, one might need to set similar parameters for overnight visitors. How long can they stay? Are guests supposed to contribute to the food bill? What about the utilities if guests are taking showers and turning on the heat and/or air-conditioning? Should they contribute? The overnight guest who becomes a permanent roommate is obviously against the lease rules.

Long-term guests can also create conflict when they interject themselves into already established roommate pairing. Interjecting opposite-sex members into same-sex roommate settings can change how everything functions in the unit, from clothing to conversations. When the overnight guest is a lover or spouse, additional dynamics occur if you are sharing a bedroom. For most tenants, the typical response is to grin and bear it—meaning that you sleep in the room you are paying for as though nothing is occurring, or else you sleep on the couch in the living room.

Roommates in college residence halls talk about arriving at their rooms to find their roommates have a guest, and a note is on the door with instructions to find somewhere else to sleep for the night. Other students describe their roommates' amorous antics as being insensitive and selfish. Either way, someone will be inconvenienced. As you can see, guests can impact the smooth running operation of the unit. They take up precious space in an already cramped living situation.

According to a Web site located in the United Kingdom entitled "Student Handbook," a recent survey conducted by students at their university highlighted ten of the things guaranteed to turn you into a basket case when sharing a unit:

- Using up the milk, butter, bread, tea, coffee, soda and not buying any more
- Pubic hair in the tub
- Ear buds by the sink
- Bathtub ring
- Not washing up
- Not buying soap, toilet paper, or dishwashing liquid

- Not cleaning the toilet
- Peeing on the floor
- The phone bill
- Band practice/choice of music
- Smelly clothes around the house
- Not having the cash to pay the rent
- Dating the roommate's new girlfriend/boyfriend

CHAPTER 6

HOUSEKEEPING

CLEANING

Cleaning is one of those things that has to be done, but usually no one wants to do it, so the dust, dirt, and dishes eventually pile up if no one takes the initiative to take on the task. The question is, who will do the cleaning? How often will it happen? And what will each of you do?

Your parents don't live there to tell you to clean up, so you and your roommates will decide when the dishes go in the dishwasher and when the toilets will be cleaned. If you decide not to clean up, no one will scream or put you on punishment unless it is your roommate and you have that kind of relationship. On the other hand, if the filth gets bad enough, the landlord can call in the department of health and cite you for unhealthy condition of the unit.

You also can be charged to clean up the unit when you leave. The best way to get cleaning under control before it gets out of control is to develop a cleaning assignment that assigns housekeeping duties to specific people on certain weeks, and post it where everyone can se it. The ideal situation is if everyone follows the cleaning chart. Realistically, however, unless one of the roommates is keeping everyone in-line, people revert to not doing their part.

One of the most repulsive sights I saw was the result of five males living in a unit for a year and never cleaning the bathroom. The bathtub was black, and the toilet was indescribable. If you clean on a weekly or biweekly basis, it will make cleaning the unit easier when you move out. If the unit is cleaned on a regular basis, there is less reason to spend three or four days cleaning the unit before you move out. Better yet, pool your money together and hire a cleaning person to come in every two weeks so things don't pile up.

Cooking and Eating

Along with cleaning, you need to decide how you will handle the cooking. If you don't like to cook, you can spend all of your money on pizza delivery. Non-students and students have an alternative to cooking, restaurants, fast food, and take-out cuisine.

Explore your local supermarket for tasty cooked food. Most supermarkets today have precooked take-out food made especially for singles. If you happen to live near a university, hospital, or any large institution, sometimes you can buy a meal plan from them and eat a decent meal at a reduced rate.

If you decide to cook in the unit, you have to decide if you will only buy food for yourself or if you will share the expenses with your roommates. The problem with sharing the food bill is that inevitably someone will eat more than his or her share of the food. Nothing is worse than going to the refrigerator for that last piece of double-chocolate cheesecake only to find someone got to it before you. Worse yet, if you share food with roommates, they might invite friends over for a feast and allow them to eat up the food you purchased for the week.

One student, describing how bad the food-stealing situation was with his roommates, said he locked his milk and cereal in his car and ate breakfast in his car at school. Eating someone else's food is a no-no. Reduce the friction of sharing food expenses by assigning everyone their own space in the kitchen cabinets and their own shelf in the refrigerator. Better yet, require everyone to pool his or her money for group grocery-shopping sessions. The positive side of sharing food expenses is that everyone can work together like a family to make meals. Consideration is the key word when sharing jointly purchased food.

ALCOHOL, PARTYING, AND DRINKING

Alcohol and partying is in no way limited to college; however, because the issue of alcohol abuse is the hottest topic on American university campuses today, I will use that as an example in this section. It seems as though when you talk about living on your own in a college town, some people think that it is synonymous with free-for-all drinking and partying. Much of that stereotype can be attributed to the movie *Animal House*, which was a celebration of drinking and college life.

Some tenants assume that the reason you get your own apartment is to have nonstop parties. The association of living on your own is synonymous with freedom. While that is true, freedom often translates into the opportunity to party when and wherever they want to. That soon grows old, after waking up with a hangover and your apartment looking like a bombed-out war zone with so many people passed out.

Students quickly learn that the remnants of nonstop partying outweigh the festivities that occurred the night before. Roommates of hard-core partying roomies describe having to deal with drunken, vomiting guests and roommates; broken furniture; fights; evictions; unwanted sexual advances; and, of course, failing grades. If your roommates are heavy drinkers and they consider you as their designated baby-sitter to get them home when they are "stone drunk," consider the liability you are taking on. In today's litigious society you could be sued if your drunken roommate injures himself or someone else while you are try-ing to get them home to sober up.

When you talk to college students who are heavy drinkers, their perception is that everyone is getting drunk. When you look closely at student behavior, however, you find that not all students are drunk on their feet. Likewise, non-students will see that not everyone is drinking; it is only a small core of very loud individuals.

You need to know what your roommate's intentions are if you want to survive. Define early in the relationship how, when, and where you and your roommate like to party. Some people don't consider it a party unless they have tapped one or two kegs (a full keg is 250 twelve-ounce cups of beer), while other people consider a few friends, a pizza, and a board game a party.

If your definition of a party is drastically different from your poten-tial roommate, you might have a conflict. It's a good idea to define the maximum number of times you are willing to tolerate partying in your unit. Do you like to party once a month, on special occasions, after finals with a few close friends, or are you an every-football-weekend-with-four-or-five-kegs-and-two-hundred-guests type of party person? Regular or constant partying can wear an individual—and his or her apartment—out.

The other part of partying that people don't address is liability. If there is a party where you live, you are liable for what occurs in your unit. If your roommate has a party where alcohol is served and minors are present, you could be fined for providing alcohol to minors and/or spend up to a year in jail, depending on the city/town regulations. Likewise, if you are under twenty-one years old and you buy, sell, or possess alcohol, you could also be fined. In the state of Pennsylvania it's an automatic $300 fine plus court costs, as well as an automatic ninety-day suspension of your driver's license. Most states have similar laws and responses to offenders. With communities and universities increas-ingly being put under pressure to deal with the behavior of underage drinkers, individuals could find themselves facing stiffer sentences for "drunk and disorderly conduct."

If you choose to entertain or have parties where alcohol is served, follow a few simple rules: (1) know who your guests are and how old they are; (2) control the flow and the intensity of the alcohol served; (3) provide nonalcoholic alternatives; and (4) do something other than drinking and getting drunk. The days of the drunken students roaming from bar to bar, stumbling home, and causing damage and vandalism along the way is slowly coming to an end. Communities are less tolerant of the obnoxious drunk who in the past was considered amusing.

In this section, I spent a great deal of time using examples of drunken students. It's important to remember that college students are merely mirrors of the greater society; therefore, whether you attend college or not, a drunken roommate is a nuisance, a liability and an embarrassment.

The media paints a slick picture of how drinking is supposed to make us more attractive to the opposite sex. The purpose of using of frogs, ferrets, lizards, and an iguana to sell beer is to make drinking look cute and amusing. Ironically, I have never seen any of these creatures drink alcohol, and, of course, if we gave these creatures the alcohol their images are used to advertise, they would end up pickled.

NOISE

At some point, when there are three or more people sharing a unit, the issue of noise will arise either by the roommates themselves toward each other or from their neighbors. At the same time, the noise might be coming from your neighbor. How do you handle it?

First, let's talk about the noise that three people can make. Depending on you and your roommates, your level of noise can be quite different from your neighbor's; likewise, your working hours might be totally different than your neighbor's. A few words of caution: Just because you like to listen to Phish and The Grateful Dead at 11:30 P.M., there is no guarantee that your neighbor will want to listen at the same time—even if they share your same taste in music. Likewise, Montovani at 8 A.M. might not be what your neighbor who works the night shift wants to hear after he or she has been in bed for only two hours. When you are renting with common walls, your neighbor almost ends up being a part of your living environment, depending on the thickness of the walls.

People who have lived on the first and second floors of a three-story building know what it is like to have someone stomping around on top of them or having the bass reverberate through the speakers on the floor through their ceiling. Please, oh please, do not put your speakers in the windows to share your music with your neighbors; that is a sure signal to get cited by the police and the landlord.

How do you deal with noise when it is not you? First of all, very carefully. My personal style is not to go to someone's door and complain that his or her noise is too loud. If that person is having a party, you might enrage forty or fifty people. In that type of situation, call your landlord and ask him or her to address it. If you decide to address the issue, address it in a non threatening way after the event, such as, "You folks really had a blowout last night. It was really rockin'; it nearly knocked me out the bed. I had to get up and go to work today with no sleep."

This is just one way of letting the individuals know you weren't happy without causing a war. If all else fails, make the confrontation the landlord's responsibility. It is a landlord's responsibility to provide quiet enjoyment—meaning, keeping the noise down at unreasonable times.

BILLS

A recurring area of conflict for tenants is the issue of who pays what bill and how much to pay. The most contentious bill is usually the telephone bill, perhaps because it is easy to identify and the easiest to abuse. Homesick and lovesick roommates can talk long-distance for hours. They don't think of the cost until they receive the bill at the end of the month. Countless hours and arguments are spent going over the bill trying to determine who called where so the charges can be fairly split.

There is no reason for tenants to have conflicts over telephone bills. A simple solution to the conflict is to have no long-distance carrier; instead, all roommates should have their own calling card for long-distance calls. Calling cards can be acquired through telephone companies or purchased at local convenience stores with a set amount of money and time on them.

Most major telephone companies have designed billing systems where roommates sharing one phone get their own personal pin numbers for billing. Each tenant receives his or her individual long-distance bill thereby reducing the conflict and making each tenant responsible for his or her bill.

For some people the telephone is a necessity; however in the dead of winter, if one has spent all the bill money on the telephone instead of the heating bill, there will be very little warmth from the telephone call to heat the unit. Prioritize, prioritize! Pay the rent; pay the utilities; extras, such as telephones, can be done without. Without a roof over your head, a telephone is a waste.

CHAPTER 7

MOVE-IN DAY

Don't Unload the Boxes Yet

It's exciting to move into a new apartment, house, or room, and most people can't wait to get settled in. However, before you run off and put flowers on the kitchen table, stop and remember that this is a business deal. Arrive at the property early, and make sure you have someone to help you unpack the vehicle or watch it while you unpack.

Before you start unloading, get the keys to the unit if you don't already have them. Check to see that the keys match the number of the unit on the lease. Then, before you unload boxes or posters, walk through the apartment. Ask the landlord for the previous tenants' checkout list. That should tell you what the landlord found wrong with the unit when those tenants left. You can use the list to determine if the landlord is giving you the unit in the same condition that he or she expects you to leave it in.

Now, get your camera, pencil, and paper, take the damage checklist found in appendix f, and begin inspecting the unit. Document the condition of the unit from top to bottom. Take pictures of the carpet, floors, ceiling, and walls of every room in the unit. This is no time to say, or think, that you can live with something just because it's not that bad. Remember that your accuracy in filling out the damage check-in list will determine how much of your security deposit is returned when you are ready to leave. It will also help to clear up any differences between you and the landlord about the condition of the unit when you moved in. If necessary, it will also be your burden of proof if you have to take the situation to court.

As you go through the rooms, check to make sure everything works. Does the toilet flush? Do the faucets turn on and off easily, or do they leak? Do the pipes leak under any of the sinks? Does the shower work? Is the refrigerator operating? Is it cold? Is the freezer functioning? Do the lights turn off and on? Do the receptacles work? If there is air-conditioning, turn it on to see if that works. Look behind and under the stove and the refrigerator. Are the areas clean?

Is the carpet clean? Are there holes or snags in any of the carpets? Note any and all of these things. If the unit has shag carpeting, look even closer at the unit; this could be an indication of the last time anything significant was done to the unit, as shag carpeting dates from the seventies.

Are there water spots on the ceiling or the walls? That can be an indication of a water leak from the roof or the pipes. Basement units and under-house garages that have been converted to apartments should be approached with caution. These units might have a tendency to flood and maintain high moisture levels, which leads to excessive mildew on anything in the unit. Look at the walls. Have they been painted? Are there spackling marks all over? What about the wallpaper? Is it dirty?

How are the windows, sliding glass doors, and the front doors? Are there visible gaps around or under the frame that let air in? If the answer is yes, you will feel those gaps when the temperature drops. Aluminum sliding doors and windows are notorious for air leaks. Are there screens on the windows? If yes, are there holes in the screens?

SAFETY NOTE

As important as a smoke detector is, tenants would do well to invest in a carbon monoxide detector also. Units heated or cooled by gas or that have gas hot-water tanks are susceptible to the pilot light going out. The result is gas leaks until someone lights the pilot light. Over the years, several students have come into the office complaining that they have experienced the effects of carbon monoxide poisoning due to the faulty, aging heating systems in the units.

CHAPTER 8

UNLIVABLE CONDITIONS

UNINHABITABLE UNITS

Tenants frequently want to know what constitutes unlivable conditions in a rental unit. Most states have statutes or laws on the books that relate to inhabitable units. In fact, Rental Housing On Line indicated that over forty-five states now impose some sort of implied warranty of habitability. What that means is if a landlord tells you that you must take the unit "as is," that is not true; an implied warranty of habitability by virtue of the intended use of the unit still exists.

Similarly, as tenants are expected to pay rent, the unit they are paying rent on has to exist. In other words, if the building burns down or floods, thus making it inhabitable, you are not obligated to pay rent if you can't use the unit. Listed below are the criteria that the Pennsylvania Landlord-Tenant Act uses to define a rental unit as inhabitable (unlivable):

- No drinkable water
- No way to lock the unit
- A broken or blocked waste disposal system (e.g., blocked sewer line)

- Poor or deficient electrical wiring (danger of fire)
- No heat in cold weather
- Unit unsafe from outside elements in cold weather
- Unit structurally unsafe plumbing, heating, windows, doors, walls, etc.
- Unit overrun with pests, roaches, and rats (in general, anything nonhuman)
- Unable to store food safely because of broken landlord-supplied refrigerator unit

Check with your particular state to find out what the rules are. The Attorney General's Office of Consumer Affairs is usually a good place to start. If the unit has any or all of these conditions, the landlord has violated the warranty of habitability. To enforce this warranty, one has to document the condition and the efforts to get the property owner to remedy the situation. In addition, one has to not be able to use the premises. The key to whether the warranty has been violated is whether the unit can be used for what it was intended. As always, document the condition and action taken with photos, letters, and names of people you talk with.

Ironically, the Bureau of the Census and the U.S. Department of Housing and Urban Development (HUD) define substandard or uninhabitable conditions a bit more severely. HUD classifies residential housing units according to whether the units have physical or structural deficiencies as follows:

- It lacks hot or cold water or a flush toilet, or both a bathtub and a shower.
- The heating equipment has broken down at least three times for six hours or more during the previous winter, resulting in the unit being uncomfortably cold for twenty-four hours or more.

- It has no electricity, or it has exposed wiring and a room with no working wall outlet and had three blown fuses or tripped circuit breakers during the previous ninety days.
- In public areas such as hallways and staircases, it has no working light fixtures, no elevator, loose or missing steps, and loose or missing railings.
- It has at least five basic maintenance problems—such as water leaks, holes in the floors or ceilings, peeling paint or broken plaster, or evidence of rats—during the previous ninety days.
- A residential housing unit is classified as having "moderate" physical problems if it does not have any of the severe problems but does have one or more of the following deficiencies: (1) on at least three occasions in the past three months, all flush toilets were broken for at least six hours; (2) un-vented gas, oil, or kerosene heaters are its primary heating equipment; (3) it lacks a sink, refrigerator, or either burners or an oven (HUD will now allow a microwave in place of a cooking stove); (4) it has three of the four hallway or staircase problems listed above; and (5) it has at least three of the basic maintenance problems listed above.

If you find any of the above-mentioned conditions, make your unit inhabitable on move in day, you shouldn't move in. Find the landlord and immediately request that the unit be cleaned or repaired at once. Do not—I repeat, do not—attempt to clean the unit or repair damages yourself. If you clean it or repair it, you have no proof of the original condition of the unit. In addition, there is no guarantee the landlord will pay you for the cleaning or repairing.

No matter how crowded the office is on move-in day, remember that you are paying for the unit to be clean when you move in. When you move out, the landlord will expect you to leave it clean, and, if you don't, they will charge you accordingly. If because of the landlord's negligence you are unable to use your unit, you should document what it means to you monetarily and ask the landlord to prorate the rent based on the fact that you were without the accommodations you paid for. Under no circumstances should you accept a unit in "as is" condition. That terminology means that you will not complain about the unit no matter what condition it is in. In most states this not acceptable

LANDLORD WON'T LET YOU MOVE IN

In the rare situation where the landlord won't allow you to move in, you need to get legal assistance. Most leases even if signed, have a clause that allows the landlord not to be held liable. If they don't have a unit for you to move into, ask the landlord why you can't move in and what unit they intended for you to move into. You need to know if the landlord is at fault or if the tenant is refusing to vacate the unit.

Because there are so many legal loopholes in this type of situation, a tenant needs an attorney to help build a strong case. If you are unable to move into your new unit, document all costs associated with not being able to move in, such as storage of possessions, interim housing, and meals. Check the lease you signed. Remember that you must have a signed lease/contract by all parties to follow up on any of these situations.

NOW YOU CAN UNLOAD THE VEHICLE

On move-in day, have someone accompany you on your move. For safety' sake, close the door of the vehicle while you unload small valuable things, such as CDs and computers. Once you are moved in, calmly survey your surroundings and look at the condition of the unit again.

For the next week, continue to take notes on the condition of the unit. If you find additional problems for the damage check-in list, send an addendum to the first one. Keep a copy of every communication you have with the landlord and his or her representatives. Without proof and documentation of the condition of the unit, you have nothing to back you up in a court of law. It's your word against the landlord's.

REPAIRS: IT'S BROKEN, BUT WHO'S GOING TO FIX IT?

There are two types of damages that usually occur in a rental unit: those that tenants cause, and those that tenants do not cause. The latter causes the greatest amount of difficulty for tenants. Getting landlords to make needed repairs in a timely fashion ranks as tenants' number-one complaint. Complaints range from no heat in the dead of winter to no hot water or air-conditioning.

Tenants complain that landlords expect them to have their rent in on time or else face fines of $5 or more per day for each day its late, yet the same landlord forgets the necessity of promptness when asked to make needed repairs on the rental unit. Landlords counter that the tenant needs to be patient and realize there are often hundreds of other tenants with similar requests.

It's important to remember that the landlord owns the property, and it's their responsibility to repair damages and *pay for them* whenever the tenant is not at fault. After the repair is made, document the condition of your unit. If the maintenance person damages or breaks something, ask them to repair it while they are in the unit. If the maintenance people refuse to rectify the situation, inform management immediately.

As a safety precaution, whenever you request maintenance, send a written copy of the request to management so that they know what maintenance is doing. In some rental companies, management does not know what maintenance is doing. If maintenance is lax in making a repair, it affects the livability of the unit; you need to let them know of the seriousness of the situation.

If the landlord tries to charge you for a repair that falls in his or her realm of responsibility, protest the charge in writing. Some landlords will attempt to take the cost of the repair out of your rent, even when you are not at fault. Some leases have a clause stating that the landlord can deduct the cost of repairs out of your rent. Do not tolerate this. Contact the local legal-aid office or your state attorney general's office of consumer affairs. Alternatively, just call your local state representative for directions on whom to call.

When requesting a repair in your unit, document the date and time of the request and to whom you reported the problem to. Don't accept problems that severely affect your living conditions for months and then expect to get a discount at the end of the lease for tolerating less-than-livable conditions. When something breaks or needs repair, let the landlord know immediately.

If you leave the object broken, assuming it's no big deal, you could be charged for it when you move out. Additionally, if the landlord walks in and finds the object broken, you could be charged. They might assume you broke the object. On the other hand, if your roommate puts his or her head through the drywall or attempts to flush a watermelon down the toilet, he or she is at fault and should pay the repair bill. If your guest damages something in the unit, you are responsible.

LANDLORD REFUSES TO MAKE REPAIRS

When the landlord won't make repairs, what should you do? Write a letter to management describing the problem and the person you communicated the problem to in the organization. If management doesn't respond, contact a consumer agency for assistance. In northern climates, a lack of heat in the unit in the dead of winter necessitates a call to landlord and, if there is no response, a call to the local code enforcement office, which in some municipalities enforces heating and cooling issues in rental units.

Frequently, tenants will ask, "Can I withhold the rent if the landlord does not make a repair?" All areas of the country have different rules and regulations regarding rent withholding. In some municipalities, if you withhold the rent, you are required to put the rent in a bank account and let the landlord know where it is. Before deciding to withhold rent, find out what the state and local rules are that cover where you live.

If you don't have the money for a lawyer, contact your state attorney general's office of consumer affairs and/or the Legal Aid Society (see Appendix J). Better yet, contact your state representative and ask him or her to send you any information pertaining to landlords' and tenants' rights and responsibilities.

CHAPTER 9

BREAKING THE LEASE AND SUBLETTING

Most landlords hold steadfastly to the rule that leases cannot be broken, and that is understandable. From a business perspective, a contract was signed and the tenant is expected to live up to their responsibility. On the other hand, there are some customer-service-oriented landlords who are more concerned with the needs of their customers. These landlords will allow the tenant to terminate the lease if adequate notice is given (usually thirty to sixty days) and the tenant pays the landlord a month's rent for the inconvenience.

Now, those of you who don't have a customer-oriented landlord are often left with few options, and you need to find out what yours are. Read your lease to determine if your landlord allows tenants to sublet. Most landlords will allow you to sublet your apartment if you pay an administrative, sublet, or break-lease fee.

The term *break-lease fee* is somewhat deceiving. It would appear that if one pays a fee of this sort, then one is theoretically out of the lease. On the contrary, in some locales the break-lease fee does nothing more than allows you to sublet your unit. You essentially pay the landlord to allow you to rent your unit. You remain responsible until the lease ends. In other parts of the country, landlords let tenants out of their lease by having the tenant give a thirty-day notice and pay one month's rent.

Who Is Responsible?

Sublets operate under the same lease rules as the original tenant. To make sure those who are subletting know the rules, provide them with a copy of the lease. If the person subletting from you damages the unit, does not pay the rent, or fails to cut the grass or shovel the snow, and it's in your lease, you are responsible. You get to be the landlord without the privileges of the profit margin. Some landlords require that the person subletting is to get in touch with the original tenant to solve problems in the unit; the original tenant then contacts the landlord. Visit the person subletting your place to inspect for damages and cleanliness in the unit to avoid surprises when the lease ends.

Subletting

In college towns that are driven by off-campus rentals, someone looking to sublet can usually get an excellent deal during the summer months. Most landlords and property owners provide only a twelve-month lease. As a result, students who leave at the end of the spring semester are faced with the prospect of staying in town and getting a job to pay for their rental unit, or leaving town and still paying for the unit.

In their rush to leave town, students sublet their units for "bargain basement prices," primarily to get some type of income for the unit while they are not occupying it. It's not unusual to hear of tenants paying $200 a month for a $400 a month apartment for the months of June, July, and half of August. No mater how good of a deal one might encounter, those who are looking to sublet need to be cautious when they find a deal that sounds too good to be true.

If you sublet, make sure the original renter has permission from the landlord to sublet the unit. There is nothing worse than thinking you have a place to live and later finding out you don't. Sublets not approved by the landlord are subject to eviction. The landlord has no obligation to the person subletting if the original tenant did not make arrangements with the landlord.

Caution also needs to be executed when paying the rent on the sublet. There have been situations where the person subletting has given the original tenant the total amount of the rent up front. A month into the lease, the new occupant learns that the original tenant did not give the money to the landlord. When this occurs the person doing the subletting is out of luck; the landlord is not obligated to let him or her stay, nor is he or she obligated to chase down the original tenant to get the rent money. The result is that the landlord can evict the person subletting for reason of nonpayment of rent and/or trespassing.

SUBLETTING AND ROOMMATES

When a roommate sublets his or her portion of the lease and doesn't take the time to introduce or inform the remaining roommates of the impending changes, this is the ingredient for a major conflict. The remaining roommates end up sharing their living accommodations with individuals they don't know. Those entering an existing roommate situation often are seen as outsiders and are treated as such.

In one situation, three women sharing a two-bedroom unit called my office expressing frustration that their roommate was subletting her space to a male none of them knew. Some landlords try to alleviate the problem of putting someone new in with existing tenants, by requiring the person doing the subletting to get the approval of all roommates before subletting the unit. Roommates have been known to reject all subletting potentials a roommate brings in, to ensure they have more room and the original tenant continues to pay the rent.

CHAPTER 10

CLEANING, MOVING OUT, SECURITY DEPOSITS, AND EVICTION

Congratulations! You survived a year or more of renting. Now let's see if you can get out with your life savings. The cleanup and the return of the security deposit are where most tenants lose the war.

If I had a dime for every tenant that has come into my office complaining about the amount of money that was taken out of his or her security deposit, I would be a millionaire. Each of these individuals always say the same thing: "We left the place in better condition than when we moved in." I ask them, "Did you document how you found the unit on move-in day with photographs and a damage checklist?" The answer is usually no, and the conversation goes downhill from there.

The only way to walk out of this portion of the rental war a winner is if you followed the advice given earlier in the book. Now, pull out the photos, the damage checklist, and all the documented complaints you made to management for maintenance or repairs. Compare that information with the unit as it stands. Contact your landlord for their checkout sheet to determine what they want cleaned. Do their cleaning requirements match the condition you found the unit on move-in day?

Good landlords will not only give you a checkout sheet, but they will also do a walk-through with you before or after you have cleaned the unit to make sure you have done a good job. Their intention is to make the rental situation a win-win experience. Now, with everything in hand, walk through the unit with a friend, and review what changed or stayed the same during your lease tenure.

CLEANING THE UNIT

The subjectivity of cleaning usually means the cleaning crew will find something they consider is not clean. It's important to remember that whenever a cleaning crew goes into a unit, the meter is ticking. It costs the landlord to have a cleaning crew come in; they need to account financially for their time. This is a business deal, and making money is the name of the game.

Tenants are not always innocent. Landlords have described—and I have seen—situations where after the tenants moved out, the unit looked like a garbage dump. One unit that I saw pictures of had garbage strewn all over the kitchen; the bathtub was black from a lack of cleaning; kitchen cabinet doors were hanging off the hinges; and bed linens and clothes were strewn all over the bedroom.

Another unit I personally inspected had so much mold in the bathroom that it had to be scraped off. The stove was so filthy that the burners were inoperable. Obviously, no security deposit could be returned. To get this unit ready for the next tenant, the landlord had to spend more than the security deposit left with them by the tenant.

Put It in the Trash

Over the years, I have had the opportunity to hear numerous horror and treasure stories about tenants who have not put the things that they do not want in the trash. Somehow, people—in their rush to vacate the premises—seem to think that the landlord or the next tenant will appreciate their leftover food in the refrigerator, cabinet, or even the oven.

No mater how well intentioned or lazy you are about not emptying those areas, you need to take the stuff to the dumpster. Even canned goods can be given to the homeless. Otherwise, you will pay for leaving them in the unit and the landlord having to cart them out.

Likewise, don't leave the never-used, filthy old couch sitting in the middle of the floor because it was too heavy to move. It has never ceased to amaze me what some tenants will leave behind. Landlords shared with me how tenants have left golf clubs, stereos, clothes, and furniture.

Let's clarify something. The landlord is not required to use his or her property as your personal storage unit once you have turned in the keys and are no longer paying rent. The landlord is obligated, in most states, to hold onto your goods for a certain amount of time if they appear salvageable. It is important to understand that each state has its own laws. Some of them indicate that if the landlord stores your goods, he or she has the right to charge you a storage fee. I would be willing to bet that they could also charge you a moving fee if they had to move your belongings to a storage area.

No doubt the worse situation I heard of was a landlady who put three young women's property out on the sidewalk. The women alleged they had confirmed with the landlady that they wanted to stay in the unit one extra day and that they would pay for the expense of doing so. The landlady, however, had a new tenant coming in right after the women, and she decided that the women's belongings needed to be out of the unit so the new tenant could move in.

The landlady allegedly paid the new tenant to move the young women's things out on the street. The result was that over $10,000 worth of personal belongings (e.g., television, camera, CDs, boom boxes, books, and clothing) were stolen off the sidewalk. The landlady's response to the accusation was that she never agreed to what the women said. Bottom line: According to the landlord-tenant law in Pennsylvania, the landlady was required to make a reasonable effort to contact the tenant to retrieve their goods. If the tenant could not be contacted and the landlady deemed the property was salvageable the landlady was required by law in Pennsylvania to put the tenant's goods in storage and charge the tenant. Check your state and region for specific rules pertaining to storage.

CLEANING COMPANIES

There appears to be three methods landlords use to get units cleaned: an independent cleaning company, in-house cleaners, and cleaning companies that are owned or operated by employees and relatives. With independent cleaning companies, the landlord gives them a list of the units that have been vacated, along with the keys, and tells them to return when they are done. The second method is when the landlord uses people from their own staff to clean the units. The third is to use cleaning companies whose staff members are related to the landlord and/or its employees.

The cleaning company's job is to find dirt to clean; that's how they get paid. Consequently, unless you document how you left the unit, they will find something to clean. It doesn't take a rocket scientist to figure out that if the cleaning company is given X number of apartments to check for cleaning, they will obviously find something to clean in each unit.

Cleaning companies are paid by the hour or the job; therefore, it is to their advantage to find something to clean in every apartment they go into. If the unit does not need to be cleaned, they obviously don't make as much money, hence the rationale for the terminology *light cleaning* and *minimum charge*. Essentially, no matter how well you clean the unit, you will be charged for the cleaning company entering your unit.

Typically in-house cleaning people work on an hourly basis for the property owner or manger. They assessed charges are as though they are an outside cleaning company. Companies that are owned by relatives, friends, or employees of the rental property would appear to, at best, be ethically suspect. No doubt the most dubious relationship between the cleaning company and the rental agent is one where the person responsible for dispersing security deposits owns the cleaning service that cleans the units.

Over the years, a problem has surfaced with landlords that use private and in-house cleaning companies. The scenario is as follows: The tenant cleans the unit and even has family members (Mom and Dad) come up to help them clean. They contact the landlord to walk through the unit with them. The tenant turns in the key to the landlord. The landlord then sends in the cleaning crew.

Sometimes the landlord looks at the unit before the cleaning crew cleans the unit; however, most of the time they take the word of the cleaning crew as to the condition of the unit. The cleaning company presents the landlord with a standard bill for services rendered. Those charges, along with an administrative handling fee, are passed on to the tenants. Details such as how much time and what specifically was cleaned are often missing from the charges. Tenants wanting those details have to write a letter to the landlord and request that they spell out what the charges are for.

This is the most blatant lack of customer service exhibited by some landlords. The same landlord who talked to the tenant and took their rent check now refuses to comment unless it's in writing. Some landlords will say that no matter how much you clean, they will send in a cleaning unit that will charge $75 minimum, whether they do anything or not.

PAINTING AND CARPET

Painting units creates a great deal of conflict between landlords and tenants. Tenants complain that they move into units that need a coat of paint, yet when they ask the landlord to paint the unit, their requests are ignored. When the tenants move out, however, they are charged for painting the unit.

Landlords and tenants need to realize that painting a unit is considered normal wear and tear. Tenants should not have to pay when it is time for the unit to be repainted. The exception is when a tenant willfully damages the paint, such as a tenant who paints a mural on the wall; or runs a mountain bike up the wall; or in any way redesigns the apartment walls or ceilings without the landlord's permission. The expense of repainting the unit is on the tenant, and the tenant can safely assume they will lose all or a portion of their security deposit. In some situations, they may even have to pay additional money.

Another familiar scenario in the rental market is charging the tenant to clean and replace the carpet at the same time. How this phenomenon occurs is that the carpet in question is beyond cleaning or repair when the tenant moves into the unit. Despite complaints from the tenant, the carpet is neither cleaned nor repaired. When the tenant moves out, the landlord charges the tenant for cleaning and replacing the carpet.

Upon receipt of the security deposit check, the tenant notes that they have been charged for not cleaning the carpet and for the replacement. When the tenant checks the unit, however, to see if the carpet has been cleaned or replaced, he or she often finds that everything is the same as it was left. Essentially nothing is done, and the tenant is double billed.

UNREALISTIC EXPECTATIONS ABOUT CLEANING

Some landlords have what I consider as an unrealistic expectation about cleaning. I sometimes even wonder, with the requirements landlords' outline for cleaning the unit, what do they do to prepare the unit for the tenants? Obviously, nothing—judging from the complaints filed by tenants regarding the condition of their unit upon moving in. Below is a list of what I consider unreasonable cleaning requests:

- Clean the kitchen and the bathroom exhaust fans.
- Disconnect the electrical wiring, and dismantle the fans and clean the blades.
- Dust lightbulbs.
- Move the stove and clean behind it.
- Take down window coverings, wash and dry them, and hang them back up (of course, if you don't hang them right, you will be charged).
- Fire extinguisher must be fully charged.
- Floor underneath the stove and the refrigerator must be scrubbed and waxed.
- Dust and scrub the baseboards.

When tenants leave the unit, they should leave it in better condition than when they found it. I am, however, concerned that many of these requirements resemble military boot camp cleaning (e.g., kitchen patrol). Tenants often move into units that were never cleaned to the specifications the landlord requires of the current tenant. Trying to clean older units is difficult at best. Rental units that have been on-line for over ten years with a steady stream of youthful tenants show their age and whether or not they have been cared for.

SOLUTION TO CLEANING WHEN YOU DON'T WANT TO

Looking in the telephone book, you can find numerous cleaning companies in your area. If you and your roommates don't want to clean the unit, contract with a cleaning service to do it for you. To ensure the cleaning specifications are in keeping with the management of your building, only contract with the people that are used by your landlord.

This, of course, will cost you. If there are four or more of you living in the unit, you could split the cost four ways. It would be interesting to see if a cleaning company would charge more than $150 to $200 to clean a unit that has not been trashed. Proceed with caution if you and your roommates have trashed the unit; you could end up paying a lot of money. If you have problems with the unit not being cleaned, you can then go after the cleaning operation for your money. Check the landlord-tenant laws in your state to determine how long the landlord has before returning your security deposit.

MOVING OUT

Once you've cleaned the unit, you want to make sure you have repaired and replaced as many items as possible. I can guarantee that if you don't replace or repair things in the unit that you are able to, you will be charged. What the landlord charges you to replace or repair will be more expensive than doing it yourself.

For instance, suppose lightbulbs cost $2 for four at Kmart or Wal-Mart. If the landlord replaces them, you will be charged $5 to $10. The same cost ratio is true for nine-volt smoke-detector batteries. When you add a 15 percent or 20 percent administrative charge to these replacements, your security deposit quickly disappears.

SECURITY DEPOSIT RETURN

After repairs, the return of security deposits is one of the largest concerns of tenants living in properties near college campuses. Their concerns are also focused on being charged exorbitant rates to replace or repair things in the unit that were already in disrepair when they moved in.

The issue of security deposits seems to bring out the worst in everyone resulting in confusion and conflict. There are several reasons for this, the most obvious being money. One way to reduce the conflict and confusion is for the landlord and tenant to document the condition of the unit at move-in and move-out time, preferably with photos. This dual documentation of the unit's condition would help to alleviate some of the security deposit conflict.

According to Rental Housing On Line, security deposits have become the most regulated issue in landlord-tenant relationships, perhaps because landlords became notorious for spending the tenants' deposits and refusing to return the money. Most state laws now contain extensive language covering how much a landlord can charge, where the money is kept, and how and when it must be returned. Some municipalities have enacted even more onerous ordinances expanding on their state law.

In most situations, security deposits can range from several hundred dollars to thousands of dollars, depending on the unit rented. The average monthly rent in 1999, according to Rental Housing On Line, was $775. When you add the first month's rent (a month ahead) with the security deposit, the average renter is putting out $2,325, leaving the tenant cash poor for the next couple of months.

The latest answer to the security deposit dilemma is security deposit insurance from Deposit Saver, a company that has designed a financial package for the landlord and the tenant to reduce the initial cash outlay for moving into a rental unit for a tenant. According to Deposit Saver, this insurance frees the tenant from the large security deposits that are normally required by most rental communities. The tenant pays a small monthly fee instead of a large cash deposit upon moving in, and the security deposit is waived altogether.

SECURITY DEPOSITS ACCORDING TO THE LAW

According to the Rental Housing On Line site, "most states require that landlords return security deposits, with a detailed list of any deductions, to the tenant within 30 days after they move out. Tenants and judges typically question landlords that provide sketchy information or statements such as general cleaning. If the landlord deducts money from your security deposit they must include valid estimates for any repairs, or the cost of those that have been done."

Questionable or exorbitant charges should be explained in detail in clear concise language. Disputes regarding security deposits invariably lead to all kinds of trouble for the landlord, the least of which may be a lawsuit. If a court finds that your landlord wrongfully withheld some or all of the security deposit because they didn't provide enough detail, or the list of deductions was returned more than thirty days after you moved out, the landlord might have to return the complete deposit to you.

In Pennsylvania, if a landlord does not return a security deposit and/or a list of charges as to why the full security deposit is not being returned, the landlord can be sued for double the amount of the security deposit. Michigan doesn't allow for cleaning to be withheld from security deposits. Check your state for the rules and regulations regarding rental housing laws and the return of the security deposit. When landlords deduct from the security deposit, it should include the following, if appropriate:

- Any unpaid utilities that are due
- A list of any damaged items or structural items and their location

- Spell out clearly the damage (e.g., four-square-foot hole in dining room wall)
- Any repairs that were made or will need to be done as result of your living there
- Cost to repair or replace items

EVICTION

Most states require that landlords clearly spell out in their lease what will get you evicted. Landlords have to follow specific procedures to evict a tenant. They can't just wake up one morning, knock on your door, and evict you. A landlord who intends to evict a tenant has to post a "notice to quit" on the tenant's door or some other obviously visible place. Essentially, this is a notice to the tenant that they are being evicted. Different areas of the country use different terminology.

Following the posting of the notice, the landlord files eviction papers with the court. Some landlords eliminate posting the notice to quit by inserting a clause in the lease that states the tenant waives the right to receive a notice to quit, which means the landlord can go directly to the court and file eviction papers.

How long the tenant has to vacate the premises depends on several factors. If you do not move out in a timely fashion, the landlord can employ the services of the sheriff. They can then forcibly evict you once the papers have been signed. Each locale has different laws, even within the state, so check with your local municipality to determine the rules and policies.

Landlords cannot, and should not, lock the door to your unit and throw your possessions on the street. That is called *self-help eviction*, and it is not allowed. A tenant can get evicted if any of the follow applies:

- The time for the lease to end is over.
- The tenant is behind in rent (does not pay the rent).
- The tenant breaks a clause in the lease.
- The landlord properly notifies you they want the property back at the end of the lease.

CHAPTER 11

UNBELIEVABLE STORIES ABOUT LANDLORDS AND TENANTS

TENANTS' STORIES ABOUT LANDLORDS

- A tenant described how a landlord refused to prorate the rent for him despite the fact that he was moving into the unit in the middle of the month. The tenant was told he had to pay a full month's rent to move in on the nineteenth. When the tenant questioned why a full month's rent, the landlord stated that their computerized accounting program did not prorate anything more than two weeks. The landlord stated to the tenant, "Why are you worried? It's such a small amount?"
- A landlord's representative encouraged and allowed two students to sign a lease without filling out a rental application to check their credit worthiness. The tenants were called a week later and told they could not move into the unit because their credit application was not approved. They would, however, have to pay rent on the unit until it was rented.

- A new student was moving into a unit with a tenant who was already in the unit. Both tenants asked the landlady if she would walk through the unit to verify the condition that the previous tenant was leaving the unit in. The landlady stated that she would not do a walk-through and that she would not give the tenants a damage checklist. In response to questions from the tenant about who would pay for the damage done by the departing tenant, the landlady responded that the new tenant would be charged for the damages done by the previous tenant. The new tenant, however, could always find the previous tenant and sue her.

- A tenant called concerned because she had signed a lease where she was responsible for paying the electricity. This was not out of the ordinary for the tenant. Upon close examination, however, she learned that she was responsible for her neighbor's use of the electricity also. When she questioned the landlord, he stated that she should split the bill with her neighbor. Upon checking with the power company, the tenant learned that the landlord's actions were illegal. The electricity was in the landlord's name, and he alone was responsible for the bill.

- Four young women lived in an apartment building for two years with no heat in one of the bedrooms, even though heat was included in the rent. The landlord gave them space heaters that ran on electricity, which they paid for. This increased the cost of their electricity bill. By the time they got to my office, they were angry because they were on their third year with no heat.

- A tenant living in a rental unit she shared with a relative of the landlord who had two extremely large dogs complained that the unit was infested with fleas. The tenant asked the landlord to de-flea the unit. The landlord's response was that she could not de-flea the unit for sixty days because the dog just had puppies.

- A tenant lived in a below ground level garage / apartment under a house. Following a torrential downpour, the tenant came home to find two feet of water in front of his door and twelve inches of water in the unit. The tenant complained to the landlord, who hesitatingly came over to make repairs. The landlord informed the tenant that he was lucky he did not charge him for the cost of pumping out the water and the cleanup as he cleared the under-sized water drain at the front door.

LANDLORDS' STORIES ABOUT TENANTS

- Tenants took it upon themselves to knock out the wall that separated the bedroom from the living room area. The tenants' rationale was that they needed a place to put the band they had invited for their party.
- Tenants painted the ceiling black and painted the solar system in fluorescent green on the ceiling.
- A tenant decided to paint a full-length wall mural on the living room wall and could not understand why the landlord was upset.
- Tenants decided to paint the hardwood floors green. They thought the color looked better than the natural color of the wood.
- Tenants paying over $600 in rent per month for a two-bedroom unit were shocked when they went to move in and the unit had spaghetti on the walls. According to the landlord, the previous tenants had so many parties that they made into *High Times* magazine for "the best place to party in State College."
- A landlord was called out of bed around 3 A.M. by the police to deal with tenants who were throwing mattresses out the second-story window and jumping on them.
- A tenant had a small party that turned into a mini riot when uninvited guests started throwing chairs out the window and fighting.

AFTERWORD

The landlord-tenant relationship is a two-way street. Most landlords and tenants perceive it as a one-way street where someone else is driving the vehicle.

What that means is tenants often think that they have no influence in the rental relationship and often expand that feeling to an "I don't care about where I am living" attitude. Some tenants think that because they are renters they are not responsible for what happens in or outside the unit. In a large rental community, that type of attitude is not acceptable or healthy. When all or some of the tenants in a rental community take an "I don't care" attitude, the facilities and the spirit of the community slowly erode.

Likewise, landlords that have the attitude that tenants are there only to pay rent find out quickly that tenants vote with their feet and voices as they leave and tell others of their negative experiences where they lived. If landlords provide customer service and treat tenants the way they would want to be treated, perhaps tenants would be more likely to treat where they live as community versus just a place to live.

ABOUT THE AUTHOR

The author Dr. Forest B. Wortham has worked in higher education, public housing and non-profit agencies for over 20 years. During that time he has written articles and presented programs to empower tenants and educate rental property owners, on tenant and landlord issues. He has also consulted with builders of multiple housing units for students in Pennsylvania and Florida.

As Assistant Director of Off Campus Living and the Student Legal Services at Penn State University he was a tenant advocate working with the 28,000 students residing off campus and over 30 local landlords. As Director of Special Programs for Fort Myers Housing Authority (Housing and Urban Development HUD) in Fort Myers Florida Dr. Wortham had the opportunity to work with rental property management staff. Dr. Wortham has a Doctorate in Adult Education from Penn State University, an ED. S in School and Community Psychology from Wayne State University and M. A. in Guidance and Counseling from the University of Detroit.

APPENDIX A

TENANT RESPONSIBILITIES

- Duty to pay rent
- Duty to pay rent, even though repairs are not done
- Duty to not abandon premises to avoid rent
- Tenant's duty to repair
- Duty to not make changes
- Duty to inform
- Duty to behave reasonably
- Duty to obey regulations
- Duty to obey the law
- Duty to observe health and building codes
- Duty to prevent waste

APPENDIX B

STATE DEADLINES FOR RETURNING SECURITY DEPOSITS

State	Deadline for Returning Security Deposit
Alabama	No statutory deadline
Alaska	14 days if the tenant gives proper notice to terminate tenancy; 30 days if the tenant does not give proper notice
Arizona	14 days
Arkansas	30 days
California	3 weeks
Colorado	1 month, unless lease agreement specifies longer period of time (which may be no more than 60 days); 72 hours if a hazardous condition involving gas equipment requires tenant to vacate
Connecticut	30 days, or within 15 days of receiving tenant's forwarding address, whichever is later
Delaware	15 days
District of Columbia	45 days

State	Deadline for Returning Security Deposit
Florida	15–45 days depending on whether tenant disputes deductions
Georgia	1 month
Hawaii	14 days
Idaho	No statutory deadline
Illinois	30–45 days depending on whether deductions were made
Indiana	45 days
Iowa	30 days
Kansas	30 days
Kentucky	30–60 days depending on whether tenant disputes deductions
Louisiana	30 days
Maine	21 days (tenancy at will) or 30 days (written rental agreement)
Maryland	30–45 days depending on whether tenant has been evicted or has abandoned the premises
Massachusetts	30 days
Michigan	30 days
Minnesota	3 weeks, or 5 days if tenant must leave due to building condemnation
Mississippi	45 days
Missouri	30 days
ntana	30 days
Nebraska	14 days
Nevada	30 days
New Hampshire	30 days
New Jersey	30 days, or 5 days in case of fire, flood, condemnation or evacuation
New Mexico	30 days
New York	Reasonable time
North Carolina	30 days

State	Deadline for Returning Security Deposit
North Dakota	30 days
Ohio	30 days
Oklahoma	30 days
Oregon	30 days
Pennsylvania	30 days
Rhode Island	20 days
South Carolina	30 days
South Dakota	2 weeks
Tennessee	No statutory deadline
Texas	30 days
Utah	30 days, or within 15 days of receiving tenant's forwarding address, whichever is later
Vermont	14 days
Virginia	30 days
Washington	14 days
West Virginia	No statutory deadline
Wisconsin	No statutory deadline
Wyoming	No statutory deadline

APPENDIX C

STATES WITH SECURITY DEPOSIT RULES (STATUTES)

Alabama	No statute
Alaska	*1 Alaska Slat. § 34.03.070
Arizona	Ariz. Rev. Slat. Ann. §§ 33-1321
Arkansas	*2 Ark- Code Ann. §§ 6-303 to -306
California	Cal. [Civil.] Code § 1950.5
Colorado	Colo. Rev. Stat. §§ 38-12-102 to -104
Connecticut	Conn. Gen. Slat. Ann. § 47a-21
Delaware	Del. Code. Ann. tit. 25, §§ 5113, 5511
District of Columbia	D.C. Code Ann. § 45 2527 and D.C. Mun. Regs. tit. 14, §§ 308-311i
Florida	Fla. Stat. Ann. § 83.49
Georgia	*3 Ga. Code Ann. §§ 44-7-30 to -36
Hawaii	Haw. Rev. Stat. § 521-44
Idaho	No statute
Illinois	*4 111. Rev. Slat. ch. 765 para. 710, 715
Indiana	Ind. Code Ann. §§ 32-7-5-1 to -19
Iowa	Iowa Code Ann. § 562AA 2

Kansas	Kan. Slat. Ann. § 58-2550
Kentucky	Ky. Rev. Slat. Ann. § 383.580
Louisiana	La. Rev. Slat. §9.3251
Maine	*5 Me. Rev. Stat. Ann. tit. 14, §§ 6031-6038
Maryland	Md. Code Ann. [Real. Prop.] § 8-203
Massachusetts	Mass. Gen. Laws Ann. ch. 186 § 15B
Michigan	Mich. Comp. Laws Ann. §§ 554.602-.613
Minnesota	Minn. Star. Ann. § 504.20
Mississippi	Miss. Code Ann. § 89-8-21
Missouri	Mo. Ann. Slat. § 535.300
Montana	Mont. Code Ann. §§ 70-25-101 to -206
Nebraska	Neb. Rev. Stat. § 76-1416
Nevada	Nev. Rev. Slat. Ann. §§ 118A.240-.250
New Hampshire	*6 N.H. Rev. Slat, Ann. §§ 540-A: 5 to : 8
New Jersey	*7 N.J. Slat. Ann. §§ 46: 8-19 to -26
New Mexico	N.M. Slat. Ann. § 47-8-18
New York	*8 N.Y. Gen. Oblig. Law §§ 7-101 to -109
North Carolina	-56 N.C. Gen. Stat. §§ 42-50 to
North Dakota	N.D. Cent. Code § 47-16-07.1
Ohio	Ohio Rev. Code Ann. § 5321.16
Oklahoma	Okla. Slat. Tit. 41 § 115
Oregon	Or. Rev. Stat. § 90.300
Pennsylvania	Pa. Stat. Ann. tit. 68, §§ 250.511 a-.512
Rhode Island	R.I. Gen. Laws § 34-18-19
South	Carolina S.C. Code Ann. § 27-40-410
South Dakota	S.D. Codified Laws Ann. §§ 43-32-6.1, -24
Tennessee	*9 Tenn. Code Ann. § 66-28-301
Texas	Tex. Prop. Code Ann. §§ 92.101-.109
Utah	Utah Code Ann. §§ 57-17-1 to -5
Vermont	Vt. Stat. Ann. tit. 9, § 4461
Virginia	Va. Code Ann. § 55-248.11
Washington	Wash. Rev, Code Ann. §§ 59.18.260 -.285

West Virginia	No statute
Wisconsin	Wisc. Admin. Code ATCP § 134-06(2)
Wyoming	No statute

* Exemptions from State Security Deposit Laws

1. Any rental unit where the rent exceeds $2,000 per month (Alaska)
2. Landlord who owns five or fewer rental units, unless these units are managed by a third party for a fee (Arkansas)
3. Landlord who owns ten or fewer rental units, unless these units are managed by an outside party (Georgia)
4. Landlord who owns four or fewer dwelling units (Illinois)
5. Rental unit, which is part of a structure with five or fewer units, one of which is occupied by landlord (Maine)
6. Landlord who leases a single-family residence and owns no other rental property, or landlord who leases rental units in an owner-occupied building of five units or less. (Exemption does not apply to any individual unit in owner-occupied building that is occupied by a person 60 years of age or older.) (New Hampshire)
7. Landlord who rents out fewer than ten rental units (New Jersey)
8. Landlord who rents out fewer than six rental units (New York)
9. Rental properties outside of Davidson, Knox, Hamilton, and Shelby Counties (Tennessee)

APPENDIX D

DEFINING WEAR AND TEAR VERSUS DAMAGES

WEAR AND TEAR
Worn-out keys
Loose or stubborn door lock
Loose hinges or handles on doors
Worn and dirty carpeting
Carpet seam unglued
Scuffed-up wood floors
Linoleum worn thin
Worn countertop
Stain on ceiling from rain or bad plumbing
Plaster cracks from settling
Faded, chipped, or cracked paint
Loose wallpaper
Balky drapery rod
Faded curtains and drapes
Heat-blistered blinds
Dirty window or door screens
Sticky window

Loose or inoperable faucet handle
Toilet runs or wobbles
Urine odor around toilet
Closet bi-fold door off track
DAMAGES
Lost keys
Broken or missing locks
Damage to a door from forced entry
Torn, stained, or burned carpeting
Rust or oil stains on carpet
Badly scratched or gouged wood floors
Linoleum with tears or holes
Burns and cuts in countertop
Stain on ceiling from overflowed tub
Holes in walls from kids or carelessness
Unapproved (bad) tenant paint job
Ripped or marked-up wallpaper
Broken drapery rod
Torn or missing curtains and drapes
Blinds with bent slats
Torn or missing screens
Broken window
Broken or missing faucet handle
Broken toilet seat or tank top
Urine or pet odor throughout unit
Damaged or missing bi-fold door

APPENDIX E

COST COMPARISON SHEET

	Unit-1	Unit-2
Studio		
One-bedroom		
Two-bedroom		
Three-bedroom		
Electricity		
Heat Efficiency		
Cable		
Parking		
Trash		
Water __Yes ___No		
Room		
House		
Cost		

APPENDIX F

DAMAGE CHECKLIST

AREAS	MOVING IN	MOVING OUT	COMMENTS
KITCHEN			
Stove			
Refrigerator			
Sink			
Disposal			
Cupboards			
Lights			
Floor/Carpet			
Ceiling			
Walls			
Closets			
Other			
LIVING ROOM			
Floor/Carpet			
Ceiling			
Walls			
Drapes			
Lights			

Closets	
Other	
DINING ROOM	
Ceiling	
Walls	
Floor/Carpet	
Lights/Furniture	
BEDROOMS	
Ceilings	
Walls	
Closets	
Floor/Carpet	
Lights/Furniture	
Other	
HALLWAYS	
Floor/Carpet	
Stairway	
Closet	
Lights	
Other	
BASEMENT	
Walls	
Ceilings	
Dryness/Humidity	
Appliances	
Heating/Cooling	
Water	
Floor	
OUTSIDE	
Sidewalks	
Porch	
Steps	

Doors, Locks, Bell
BASEMENT
Walls
Ceilings
Dryness/Humidity
Appliances
Heating/Cooling
Water
Floor
Other
OUTSIDE
Sidewalks
Porch
Steps
Doors, Locks, Bell
Other
BATHROOM
Toilet

AREAS	MOVING IN	MOVING OUT	COMMENTS
Sink/Cabinet			
Tub/Shower			
Walls/Tiles			
Floor			
Ceiling			
Exhaust Fan			
Lights			
Closet			
OTHER			
Pool			
Jacuzzi			
Lanai			
Lighting			
Screens			
Windows			

Moving In   Moving Out

Tenant _____ Tenant _____

Landlord_____ Landlord _____

Date _____ Date _____

APPENDIX F

DAMAGE CHECKLIST

AREAS	MOVING IN	MOVING OUT	COMMENTS
KITCHEN			
Stove			
Refrigerator			
Sink			
Disposal			
Cupboards			
Lights			
Floor/Carpet			
Ceiling			
Walls			
Closets			
Other			
LIVING ROOM			
Floor/Carpet			
Ceiling			
Walls			
Drapes			
Lights			

Closets
Other
DINING ROOM
Ceiling
Walls
Floor/Carpet
Lights/Furniture
BEDROOMS
Ceilings
Walls
Closets
Floor/Carpet
Lights/Furniture
Other
HALLWAYS
Floor/Carpet
Stairway
Closet
Lights
Other
BASEMENT
Walls
Ceilings
Dryness/Humidity
Appliances
Heating/Cooling
Water
Floor
OUTSIDE
Sidewalks
Porch
Steps
Doors, Locks, Bell

BASEMENT			
Walls			
Ceilings			
Dryness/Humidity			
Appliances			
Heating/Cooling			
Water			
Floor			
Other			
OUTSIDE			
Sidewalks			
Porch			
Steps			
Doors, Locks, Bell			
Other			
BATHROOM			
Toilet			

AREAS	MOVING IN	MOVING OUT	COMMENTS
Sink/Cabinet			
Tub/Shower			
Walls/Tiles			
Floor			
Ceiling			
Exhaust Fan			
Lights			
Closet			
OTHER			
Pool			
Jacuzzi			
Lanai			
Lighting			
Screens			
Windows			

Moving In   Moving Out
Tenant _____Tenant _____
Landlord_____Landlord _____
Date _____Date _____

APPENDIX G

COLLEGE STUDENT ROOMMATE COMPATIBILITY QUESTIONNAIRE

1. How many hours a day do you spend studying
   A. at home?   B. at the library?
2. What's your major?
3. Which of the following do you study with?
   A. soft music
   B. hard-rock music
   C. television on
   D. heavy-metal music
   E. absolute silence
   F. rap or hip-hop music
4. Do you work?
   Yes   No
   If yes, how many hours a week?
5. Do you smoke cigarettes?
   Yes   No
   If yes,   1/2 pack day? 1-2 packs/day? 3-5 packs/day?

6. Do you drink?

Yes   No

If yes, 1-2 drinks at a party? 6-pack a night? drink to get drunk?

7. Do you approve of drugs?

Yes   No

8. Do you like to party?

Yes   No

If yes, how many hours a week? 1-5 hours 6-10 hours 10-20 hours

9. Do you mind if roommates have overnight guests?

Yes (explain)   No

If yes how many days/nights?

10. Are you messy or very neat?

11. When angry, do you do any of the following?

A. talk to people

B. hit things

C. hit people

D. get drunk

12. Do you have children?

Yes   No

If yes, how many?

13. If you answered yes above, will they visit you?

Yes   No

This questionnaire in no way guarantees a match between you and your future roommate(s). Rather, it is to be used as a discussion tool to help you explore your similarities and dissimilarities. As in any living relationship, people and situations change; therefore, it is imperative that roommates talk out their differences.

Appendix H

Roommate Compatibility Questionnaire

1. Do you work?

   Yes   No

   If yes, how many hours a week?

2. How many hours a day do you spend at home?

3. Do you smoke cigarettes?

   Yes   No

   If yes, explain. 1/2 pack/day 1-2 packs/day 3-5+ packs/day

4. Do you drink?

   Yes   No

   If yes, explain. 1-2 drinks at a party 6-pack a night drink to get drunk

5. How do you usually spend your time at home?

   A. listening to soft music

   B. listening to hard-rock music

   C. watching television

   D. listening to heavy-metal music

   E. in absolute silence

   F. listening to rap music

   G. entertaining my significant other

6. Do you smoke cigarettes?

Yes   No

If yes, how many? 1/2 pack day 1-2 packs/day 3-5 packs/day

7. Do you approve of drugs?

Yes   No

8. Do you like to party?

Yes   No

If yes, how many hours a week? 1-5 hours 6-10 hours 10-20 hours

9. Do you mind if roommates have overnight guests?

Yes (explain) No

How many days/nights?

10. Are you messy or very neat?

11. When angry, do you do any of the following?

A. talk to people   B. hit things   C. hit people   D. get drunk

12. Do you have children?

Yes   No

If yes, how many?

13. If you answered yes above, will they visit you and how often?

Yes   No

This questionnaire in no way guarantees a match between you and your future roommate(s). Rather, it is to be used as a discussion tool to help you explore your similarities and dissimilarities. As in any living relationship, people and situations change; therefore, it is imperative that roommates talk out their differences.

APPENDIX I

Roommate Agreement

- Rent total amount
- Rent per person
- Basic telephone services
- Per person basic telephone
- Cable Services
- Per person
- Agreement to share electric bill (initial)
- Agreement to share water bill (initial)
- Agreement to share gas bill (initial)
- Cost of trash pick-up
- Per person cost for trash pick up
- Housekeeping Responsibilities
- Kitchen
- Bathroom
- Common areas i.e. living room, dining room den etc.
- Grass mowing Shoveling snow

Name   Drivers License #

Name   Drivers License #

APPENDIX J

LANDLORD/TENANT RESOURCES IN THE UNITED STATES

ALABAMA

Alabama Landlord-Tenant Law
Address: 207 Montgomery St., Suite 725, Montgomery, AL 36104-3561
Phone: (334) 263-4663
E-mail: cafhc@mindspring.com
Web site: http://www.legislature.state.al.us/codeofalabama/1975/135724.htm

Attorney General's Office, Consumer Affairs Division
Address: 11 S. Union St., Montgomery, AL 36130
Phone: (334) 242-7374
Fax: (334) 242-2433
Web site: http://www.ago.state.al.us/

Mobile Fair Housing Center
Address: 951 Government Blvd., Suite 827, Mobile, AL 36604-2430
Phone: (334) 433-8070

Fax: (334) 433-8073
E-mail: mfhcinc@aol.com
Web site: http://www.fairhousing.com/mfhc/

ALASKA

Alaska Department of Law (Attorney General's Office)
Available documents include the Uniform Residential Landlord and Tenant Act
Address: P.O. Box 110300, Juneau, AK 99811-0300
Phone: (907) 465-3600
Fax: (907) 465-2075
E-mail: Attorney_General@law.state.ak.us
Web site: http://www.law.state.ak.us/

Alaska Legal Services
Serves low-income tenants only. If you're being evicted, be sure you mention the eviction when you call this company. There are several offices; see their Web site for complete contact information.
Web site: http://www.ptialaska.net/~aklegal/

The Landlord and Tenant Act: What It Means to You
Produced by the Alaska Real Estate Commission in cooperation with the Alaska Department of Law.
Web site: http://www.dced.state.ak.us/occ/landlord.htm

ARIZONA

Arizona Association of Manufactured Home Owners, Inc.
Represents manufactured home and RV owners in Arizona. Services include lobbyists at the state and local levels of government; workshops; legal assistance fund; and mediation between landlord and tenant.

Address: 2334 S. McClintock Dr., Tempe, AZ 85282-2674
Phone: (602) 966-9566 or (800) 221-6955
Fax: (602) 966-0442

Arizona Tenants Association
Provides information about tenant rights; has a legal assistance program.
Address: 1818 S. 16th St., Phoenix, AZ 85034-5304
Phone: (602) 257-8987
Fax: (602) 257-9323

Overview of Arizona Residential Landlord-Tenant Law
From the Arizona Supreme Court's Public Information Office
Web site: http://www.supreme.state.az.us/info/landlord.htm

Phoenix (city of) Human Services Department (HSD) Sky Harbor Family Services Center
Address: 1818 S. 16th St., Phoenix, AZ 85034-5304
Phone: (602) 495-5193
Fax: (602) 534-2786
E-mail: jherst@ci.phoenix.az.us

ARKANSAS

Arkansas Attorney General's Office, Consumer Protection Division
They publish a tip sheet on landlord/tenant rights.
Address: 200 Catlett-Prien Tower, 323 Center St., Little Rock, AR 72201
Phone: (501) 682-2341(800) 482-8982
E-mail: consumer@ag.state.ar.us
Web site: http://www.ag.state.ar.us/consumer/

Arkansas Landlord-Tenant Statutes
The Arkansas Legislature Web site has landlord-tenant statutes available on-line.

Arkansas Fair Housing Council
Address: 708 Clinton St., Suite 107, Arkadelphia, AR 71923-5900
Phone: (870) 245-3855

CALIFORNIA

Berkeley Rent Stabilization Board
Address: 2125 Milvia St., Berkeley, CA 94704-1112
Phone: (510) 644-6128
TTY: (510) 644-7703
Fax: (510) 644-6915
E-mail: rent@ci.berkeley.ca.us
Web site: http://www.ci.berkeley.ca.us/rent/

Berkeley Tenant Action Project (TAP)
A paralegal group that does tenant counseling and emergency work.
Address: 2022 Blake St., Room E, Berkeley, CA 94704-2604
Phone: (510) 843-6601

Beverly Hills Rent Control Hot Line
Address: 455 N. Rexford Dr., Beverly Hills, CA 90210
Phone: (310) 285-1031

California Tenants: A Guide to Residential Tenants' and Landlords' Rights and Responsibilities
Provided by the California Department of Consumer Affairs. Paper copies are available for a small fee.
Web site: http://www.dca.ca.gov/legal/landlordbook/

CalPIRG Renters' Guide
Web site: http://www.pirg.org/calpirg/consumer/renters/index.htm

Coalition for Economic Survival
Organizes tenants in Los Angeles and West Hollywood.
Address: 1296 N. Fairfax Ave., Los Angeles, CA 90046-5206
Phone: (323) 656-4410
Fax: (323) 656-4416
E-mail: ces@loop.com **Foxridge Apartments Tenants Union (FTU)**
Address: 3715 Tallyho Dr., Apt. 133, Sacramento, CA 95826-5470

Legal Aid Society of San Diego
Provides legal services to poor residents of San Diego city and county.
Branch office in Oceanside.
Address: 110 S. Euclid Ave., San Diego, CA 92114-3796
Phone: (619) 262-5557
Fax: (619) 263-5697
E-mail: ajabum@lassd.org

Los Angeles County Department of Consumer Affairs
Provides information on state law regarding renting units in California, repair and rent deduction, habitability, moving out, security deposits, retaliatory evictions, rental agreements, abandonment, and the protection of privacy.
Address: 500 W. Temple St., Room B-96, Los Angeles, CA 90012-2706
Phone: (213) 974-1452
E-mail: rent@ci.berkeley.ca.us
Web site: http://consumer-affairs.co.la.ca.us/toc.htm

Los Angeles Housing Department
Publishes a landlord-tenant handbook, available to the public for free by request. For Los Angeles residents, these are the people to call about rent stabilization, rent reduction, rent escrow, and urgent repairs.
Address: 400 S. Main St., Los Angeles, CA 90013
Phone: (213) 847-RENT
Web site: http://www.ci.la.ca.us/LAHD/

San Francisco Rent Board
Address: 25 Van Ness Ave., Suite 320, San Francisco, CA 94102-6033
Phone: (415) 252-4600
Fax: (415) 252-4699
E-mail: Rent_Board@ci.sf.ca.us
Web site: http://www.ci.sf.ca.us/rentbd/index.htm

San Francisco Tenants Union (SFTU)
Provides tenant counseling, organizing, and lobbying. The SFTU is an established and respected institution.
Address: 558 Capp St., San Francisco, CA 94110-2516
Phone: (415) 282-6622
Fax: (415) 282-6622
E-mail: sftu@slip.net
Web site: http://www.sftu.org/

Santa Monicans for Renters Rights
Address: Santa Monica, CA
E-mail: info@smrr.org
Web site: http://www.smrr.org/

Santa Monica Rent Control Board
Address: 1685 Main St., Room 202, Santa Monica, CA 90401
Phone: (310) 458-8751
E-mail: rent-control@ci.santa-monica.ca.us
Web site: http://pen.ci.santa-monica.ca.us/rentcontrol/

SF Renter
An independent on-line guide for San Francisco tenants.
Address: San Francisco, CA
Web site: http://www.sfrenter.com/

Tenants' Rights Union of Santa Cruz
Address: P.O. Box 7484, Santa Cruz, CA 95061-7484
Phone: (408) 426-0644
E-mail: tenantsrights@cruzers.com
Web site: http://www.cruzers.com/~tenantsrights/

The Tenants Legal Center of San Diego
A community law office in San Diego. Attorneys provide low-cost legal assistance to residential tenants.
Address: 5252 Balboa Ave., Suite 408, San Diego, CA 92117-6939
Office phone: (858) 571-7100
Recorded landlord/tenant information: (858) 571-1166
E-mail: info@tenantslegalcenter.com
Web site: http://www.tenantslegalcenter.com/

West Hollywood Rent Stabilization Department
Address: West Hollywood, CA
Phone: (323) 848-6450
Web site: http://www.ci.west-hollywood.ca.us/rsd/

COLORADO

Boulder Community Mediation Service
This service provides information to Boulder residents about landlord/ tenant rights and responsibilities. You can request to have a mediator assigned to help you resolve landlord-tenant, roommate-roommate, and neighbor-neighbor problems. The service is part of Boulder's Department of Housing and Human Services. They also publish a landlord-tenant handbook similar to the *Boulder Tenants Guide*.
Address: 2160 Spruce St., Boulder, CO

Phone: (303) 441-4364

Boulder Community Network Housing Center
This Web page is packed with information about local housing author-
ities, low-income housing assistance, resources, and renters' resources.
Address: Boulder, CO
E-mail: echelmei@bcn.boulder.co.us
Web site: http://bcn.boulder.co.us/housing/

Boulder Tenants Guide
A project of off-campus student services at the University of Colorado
at Boulder.
Address: Boulder, CO
Web site: http://www.colorado.edu/OCSS/indextenant.html

Colorado Statute Manager
Allows search access to the 1999 Colorado Statutes and Court Rules. For
landlord/tenant information, look up Title 38, Article 12 by entering
"38-12" in the "Statutes by Number" page.
Web site: http://165.212.243.216/stat99/

Housing Advocacy Coalition
Address: P.O. Box 434, Colorado Springs, CO 80901-0434

Housing Information and Community Referral
Provides information and referrals to Denver residents on housing
problems such as questions about lease agreements, security deposits,
evictions, and locating affordable and emergency housing.
Address: 1905 Sherman St., Suite 920, Denver, CO 80203
Office phone: (303) 831-1750
Landlord/tenant information: (303) 831-1935
TTY: (303) 831-0485:
Fax: (303) 831-0599

Landlord/Tenant Counseling—Jeffco Action Center
Helps landlords and tenants in the Denver metro area. Explains tenant and landlord legal rights, makes suggestions about disputes, and provides counseling in dealing with government assistance programs.
Address: 8755 W. 14th Ave., Lakewood, CO 80215-4895
Phone: (303) 237-7704 or (303) 237-0230
Fax: (303) 237-6002

Landlord/Tenant Counseling—Legal Aid Society (Denver)
Provides legal information and counseling about landlord-tenant disputes to low-income people and seniors living in the metro Denver area.
Address: 1905 Sherman St., Suite 400, Denver, CO 80203-1181
Phone: (303) 837-1321

State of Colorado Civil Rights Division
Enforces Colorado's civil rights laws, which prohibit certain forms of discrimination in housing, employment, and public accommodations.
Address: 1560 Broadway, Suite 1050, Denver, CO 80202-4941
E-mail: jack.lym@state.co.us
Web site: http://www.dora.state.co.us/Civil-Rights/

CONNECTICUT

Connecticut Landlord-Tenant Law
Web site: http://www.cslnet.ctstateu.edu/statutes/title47a/httoc.htm

Connecticut Fair Housing Center
Address: 221 Main St., Hartford, CT 06106
Phone: (860) 247-4400 or (888) 247-4401
Fax: (860) 247-4326

The ConnPIRG Guide to Tenant Rights and Responsibilities
Web site: http://www.pirg.org/connpirg/consumer/renters/index.htm

DELAWARE

Delaware Attorney General's Office
They have several branch offices around the state.
E-mail: Attorney.General@State.DE.US
Web site: http://www.state.de.us/attgen/index.htm

Delaware Landlord-Tenant Code Summary
Web site: http://www.grmco.com/html/landlord_-_tenant.html

DISTRICT OF COLUMBIA

D.C. Department of Consumer and Regulatory Affairs
Address: 614 H St. NW, Washington, DC 20001
Phone: (202) 727-7395
Web site: http://www.dcra.org/

D.C. Tenants Advocacy Coalition (TENAC)
Assists tenants through education, legal assistance, lobbying for pro-tenant legislation, and forming tenant associations in rental buildings.
Address: P.O. Box 7237, Washington, DC 20044
Phone: (202) 628-3688

Fair Housing Council of Greater Washington
Address: 1212 New York Ave. NW, Suite 500, Washington, DC 20005
Phone: (202) 289-5360

Landlord and Tenant Consult Service
A service of the city of Washington, D.C.
Address: Washington, DC 20001
Phone: (202) 879-1157

FLORIDA

Florida's Office of Attorney General
Address: The Capitol, Tallahassee, FL 32399-1050
Phone: (850) 487-1963
Fax: (850) 487-2564
Web site: http://legal.firn.edu/

Florida PIRG's Renters' Rights Handbook
Web site: http://www.pirg.org/pirg/floridapirg/consumer/renters/rrpage1.htm

Florida Residential Landlord and Tenant Act
Web site:
http://www.leg.state.fl.us/citizen/documents/statutes/1997/ch0083/PA
RT02.HTM

Three Rivers Legal Services
Provides free civil legal services to low-income, eligible clients in twelve counties of North Central Florida. Branch office in Lake City. Staff members regularly travel to meet with clients in the other counties served.
Address: 111 S.W. 1st St., Gainesville, FL
Phone: (352) 372-0519 (800) 372-0936
Web site: http://www.trls.org/

GEORGIA

Atlanta Legal Aid Society, Inc. (ALAS)
Many locations. The ALAS publishes many tenancy-related community education brochures and works with tenants and tenant groups through its housing program.
Address: 151 Spring St. NW, Atlanta, GA 30303-2097
Phone: (404) 524-5811
TTY: call the Georgia Relay Center at (800) 255-0056
Fax: (404) 525-5710
Web site: http://www.law.emory.edu/PI/ALAS/

Georgia Landlord/Tenant Hot Line
Address: P.O. Box 79072, Atlanta, GA 30357-7072
Phone: (404) 206-5343 or (800) 369-4706

HAWAII

Hawaii Office of Consumer Protection (OCP)
Publishes the *Hawaii Landlord-Tenant Handbook*. The OCP has various branch offices. See http://www.hawaii.gov/dcca/ocp/hours.html for locations and hours.
Address: 235 S. Beretania St., Suite 801, Honolulu, HI 96813-2419
Phone: (808) 586-2634 (800) 513-8886
Fax: (808) 586-2640
E-mail: ocp@counsel.com
Web site: http://www.hawaii.gov/dcca/ocp/

Hawaii Residential Landlord-Tenant Handbook
Provided by the State of Hawaii Office of Consumer Protection.
Web site: http://www.hawaii.gov/dcca/ocp/Landlord.html

IDAHO

Idaho Attorney General's Office, Consumer Protection Unit
Address: 700 W. Jefferson St., P.O. Box 83720, Boise, ID 83720-0010
E-mail: jlanham@ag.state.id.us
Web site: http://www2.state.id.us/ag/consumer/consumer.htm

Idaho Citizens Network
Address: 1311 W. Jefferson Ave., Boise, ID 83702-5320
Phone: (208) 385-9146

Idaho Landlord-Tenant Guidelines
Prepared by Idaho's office of attorney general.
Web site: http://www2.state.id.us/ag/consumer/tips/landman.htm

ILLINOIS

Chicago HUD Alliance for Tenants
Address: 4550 N. Clarindon, Suite D, Chicago, IL 60640

Chicago's Metropolitan Tenants Organization
Address: 2125 W. North Ave., Chicago, IL 60647
Phone: (312) 292-4980
Fax: (312) 292-0333
E-mail: mto@cnt.org
Web site: http://www.cnt.org/~mto/

Illinois Tenants Union
Helps tenants with breaking a lease, paying reduced rent due to unmade repairs, getting security deposits returned, finding legal representation for tenants facing eviction, etc.
Address: 4616 North Drake, Chicago, IL 60625-5814

Phone: (773) 478-1133
Web site: http://www.tenant.org/

Landlord and Tenant Fact Sheet
From the office of the attorney general.
Web site: http://www.ag.state.il.us/publications/landlord.html

Metropolitan St. Louis Equal Housing Opportunity Council
A private, not-for-profit fair housing enforcement agency working to end illegal housing discrimination. Serves anyone in the Missouri counties of St. Louis, St. Charles, Franklin, and Jefferson, as well as the city of St. Louis; and in the Illinois counties of St. Clair, Madison, and Monroe.
Address: 1027 S. Vandeventer Ave., Fourth Floor, St. Louis, MO 63110-3805
Phone: (314) 534-5800 (800) 555-3951
TTY: (800) 735-2966
Fax: (314) 534-2551
E-mail: ehoc@stlouis.missouri.org
Web site: http://stlouis.missouri.org/501c/ehoc/

The Tenant Union at Champaign-Urbana
A resource for all renters in Champaign-Urbana. University of Illinois students can visit the Tenant Union at C-U in the Illini Union, Room 326.
Address: 44 E. Main St., Suite 208, Champaign, IL 61820-3636
Phone for all tenants: (217) 352-6220
Phone for University of Illinois students only: (217) 333-0112
E-mail: tenant@uiuc.edu
Web site: http://www.uiuc.edu/ph/www/tenant/

INDIANA

Indiana's Office of the Attorney General
Address: State House, Room 219, Indianapolis, IN 46204-2731
Main office: (317) 232-6201

Consumer protection division: (800) 382-5516
E-mail: constituent@atg.state.in.us
Web site: http://www.state.in.us/attorneygeneral/

IOWA

Iowa Coalition for Housing and Homeless
Provides technical assistance, community organizing, and public policy advocacy around housing and homeless issues.
Address: 713 E. Locust St., Des Moines, IA 50309-1915
Phone: (515) 288-5022
E-mail: coydo@yahoo.com

Linn County Mobile Home Tenants Association
Address: P.O. Box 8381, Cedar Rapids, IA 52408-8381
Phone: (319) 390-7132

KANSAS

Housing and Credit Counseling, Inc.
Provides walk-in or call-in counseling and publishes information for tenants on its Web site.
Address: 1195 S.W. Buchanan, Suite 203, Topeka, KS 66604-1183
Phone: (785) 234-0217 or (800) 383-0217
Fax: (785) 234-0237
E-mail: hcci@hcci-ks.org
Web site: http://www.hcci-ks.org/

Kansas Attorney General's Office
Publishes a page on landlord/tenant rights and obligations.
Address: 301 S.W. 10th Ave., Topeka, KS 66612

Phone: (785) 296-2215
E-mail: GENERAL@at01po.wpo.state.ks.us
Web site: http://www.ink.org/public/ksag/main.htm

The Legal Aid Society of Topeka
Provides legal advice and representation to low-income residents of Shawnee, Douglas, Osage, Jefferson, Jackson, Atchison, Morris, and Wabaunee Counties.
Address: 712 S. Kansas, Suite 200, Topeka, KS 66603-3873
Phone: (785) 354-8531
TTY: (785) 233-4028
Fax: (785) 233-2096

KENTUCKY

Kentucky Attorney General's Office
Address: 1024 Capital Center Dr., Frankfort, KY 40601
Phone: (502) 696-5389
E-mail: attorney.general@law.state.ky.us
Web site: http://www.law.state.ky.us/

Louisville Tenants' Union, Inc.
Address: 425 W. Muhammad Ali Blvd., Louisville, KY 40202
Phone: (502) 587-0287

LOUISIANA

Louisiana Department of Justice, Consumer Protection Section
Publishes a landlord/tenant fact sheet.
Address: State Capitol, 22nd Floor, Baton Rouge, LA 70804-9005
Phone: (800) 351-4889

Fax: (504) 342-7335
E-mail: info@laag.com
Web site: http://www.laag.com/conpro.cfm

Louisiana Fair Housing Information
A service of the attorney general's office.
Phone: (800) 273-5718
Web site: http://www.laag.com/equalho.cfm

MAINE

Consumer Rights When You Rent an Apartment
Part of the *Maine Attorney General's Consumer Law Guide.*
Web site: http://www.state.me.us/ag/clg14.htm

Pine Tree Legal Assistance
A nonprofit corporation providing legal assistance to people in Maine whose income is 125 percent of the federal income poverty guidelines or less. Many office locations.
Web site: http://www.ptla.org/

MARYLAND

Baltimore Neighborhoods, Inc.
Address: 2217 Saint Paul St., Baltimore, MD 21218-5806
Tenant/landlord information: (410) 243-6007
Long distance within Maryland: (800) 487-6007
Fair housing: (410) 243-4400
Mobility/organizing: (410) 243-4485
Administration: (410) 243-4468
Web site: http://www.clark.net/pub/mmark/bni2.html

Legal Aid Bureau, Inc.
Many offices throughout Maryland.
Address: 500 East Lexington St., Baltimore, MD 21202
Phone: (410) 539-5340 (800) 999-8904
TTY: (800) 485-5340
Fax: (410) 539-1710
Web site: http://www.mdlab.org/

Takoma Park Renters Information
Prepared by Takoma Park's Department of Housing and Community
Development.
Web site: http://www.cityoftakomapark.org/dhcd/

MASSACHUSETTS

Anti-Displacement Project
Organizes tenants in at-risk housing in western Massachusetts.
Address: 57 School St., Springfield, MA 01105-1331
Phone: (413) 739-7233
Fax: (413) 746-8862
E-mail: adp@javanet.com

Legal Services for Cape Cod and Islands, Inc. (LSCCI)
Serves the legal needs of low-income and elderly residents of Cape Cod,
Martha's Vineyard, Nantucket, and eastern Plymouth County. The LSCCI
Housing Unit helps clients facing lockouts, evictions, discrimination, and
termination from public housing programs, utility shutoffs, and poor
housing conditions. The site includes a page on deposits and fees.
Address: 460 West Main St., Hyannis, MA 02601
Hyannis: (800) 742-4107
Plymouth: (800) 585-4933
E-mail: lscci@lscci.org
Web site: http://www.lscci.org

Massachusetts Alliance of HUD Tenants
Address: 353 Columbus Ave., Boston, MA 02116-6005
Phone: (617) 267-2949
Fax: (617) 267-4769
E-mail: tenant_alliance@juno.com

Massachusetts Tenants Organization
Address: 14 Beacon St., Boston, MA 02108
Phone: (617) 367-6628
Fax: (617) 720-5384

Tenant Information from Massachusetts Legal Services
Includes information about eviction, housing conditions, fair housing, and subsidized housing, as well as excellent information about Massachusetts tenants' rights in general.
Web site: http://www.neighborhoodlaw.org/housing.htm

The Central Massachusetts Housing Alliance
Address: 7 Bellevue St., Suite 11, Worcester, MA 01609-1801
Phone: (508) 791-7265
Fax: (508) 791-0639
E-mail: cmha@ultranet.com
Web site: http://www.ultranet.com/~cmha/

MICHIGAN

Ann Arbor Tenants Union
Address: 4315 Michigan Union, Ann Arbor, MI 48109
Phone: (734) 763-6876
E-mail: aatu@umich.edu
Web site: http://www.umich.edu/~aatu/

Housing Resource Center
Address: 300 Bailey St., Room 301, East Lansing, MI 48823-4444
Phone: (517) 337-9795

Michigan Attorney General
Publishes various helpful Web pages on landlord-tenant relations.
Address: P.O. Box 30213, Lansing, MI 48909-7713
Phone: (517) 373-1140
Web site: http://www.ag.state.mi.us/

United Community Housing Coalition
Address: 47 E. Adams Ave., Suite 201, Detroit, MI 48226-1681
Phone: (313) 963-3218

MINNESOTA

Community Stabilization Project
Organizes tenants around issues of affordable housing.
Address: 671 Selby Ave., Suite B, St. Paul, MN 55104-6668
Phone: (651) 225-8778
Fax: (651) 225-9820

Duluth Tenants Union
Provides information and advocacy to renters.
Address: 206 W. 4th St., Suite 212, Duluth, MN 55806-2713
Phone: (218) 722-6808
Fax: (218) 722-0375

Landlords and Tenants: Rights and Responsibilities
Published by the Minnesota attorney general's office.
Web site: http://www.ag.state.mn.us/home/consumer/housing/land-
lordtenant/default.html

Minnesota Tenants Union (MNTU)
Their main work is individual tenant advocacy. The MNTU also does some public policy work, media work, and limited tenant organizing.
Address: 610 W. 28th St., Minneapolis, MN 55408-2101
Phone: (612) 871-7485 or 900-225-8888 (fee for call)
Fax: (612) 871-2701

Project 504
Works to prevent the loss of affordable rental housing in the Phillips neighborhood of Minneapolis. Project 504 organizes tenants in substandard housing and, in appropriate cases, brings court action to improve the housing.
Address: 1113 E. Franklin Ave., Suite 309, Minneapolis, MN 55404
Phone: (612) 277-0408
Fax: (612) 277-0409
E-mail: gluce@project504.org
Web site: http://www.project504.org

St. Paul Tenants Union
A nonprofit, membership-based organization that provides information and technical assistance to tenants, educates the public about tenant rights, and organizes low-income tenants.
Address: 500 Laurel Ave., St. Paul, MN 55102-2020
Phone: (651) 221-0501
Fax: (651) 222-0931

StarTribute Home Zone—Renting
This site features an "ask the experts" forum on tenants issues, as well as lots of other information about renting in Minnesota.
Web site: http://www.startribune.com/homezone/rent/

The Landlord and Tenant Information Help Line
Serves all of Minnesota.
Address: 1421 Park Ave., Suite 100, Minneapolis, MN 55404
Phone: (612) 341-3504
Fax: (612) 341-3160 (Landlord and Tenant Housing Information Fax
Request System)

MISSISSIPPI

Mississippi Residential Landlord-Tenant Act
Web site: http://www.mscode.com/free/statutes/89/008/index.htm

MISSOURI

Housing Comes First
A Missouri citizens' coalition working to preserve housing and neigh-
borhoods for people with low and moderate incomes.
Address: 5300 Delmar, St. Louis, MO 63112-3199
Phone: (314) 367-2993
Fax: (314) 367-9626
E-mail: hcf@stlouis.missouri.org
Web site: http://stlouis.missouri.org/501c/hcf/

Metropolitan St. Louis Equal Housing Opportunity Council
A private, not-for-profit fair housing enforcement agency working to end
illegal housing discrimination. Serves anyone in the Missouri counties of
St. Louis, St. Charles, Franklin, and Jefferson, as well as the city of St.
Louis; and in the Illinois counties of St. Clair, Madison, and Monroe.
Address: 1027 S. Vandeventer Ave., Fourth Floor, St. Louis, MO 63110-3805
Phone: (314) 534-5800 (800) 555-3951
TTY: (800) 735-2966

Fax: (314) 534-2551
E-mail: ehoc@stlouis.missouri.org
Web site: http://stlouis.missouri.org/501c/ehoc/

MONTANA

Montana People's Action
Offices in Missoula, Billings, and Bozeman.
Address: 208 E. Main St., Missoula, MT 59802
Phone: (406) 728-5297
Fax: (406) 728-4095
Web site: http://www.mtpaction.org/

NEBRASKA

Fair Housing Center of Nebraska
Address: 522 N. 24th St., Omaha, NE 68110
Phone: (402) 444-6675

Legal Aid Society [Nebraska]
Dedicated to meeting the civil legal needs of impoverished people. It conducts clinics on landlord-tenant law, counsels and represents low-income tenants, and publishes a Nebraska landlord-tenant guide.
Address: 500 S. 18th St., Suite 300, Omaha, NE 68102
Phone: (402) 348-1069
Fax: (402) 348-1068
E-mail: jawagner@las-omaha.org
Web site: http://www.las-omaha.org/

Nebraska Attorney General's Office, Consumer Protection Division
Address: 2115 State Capitol Building, Lincoln, NE 68509
Main office: (402) 471-2682

Consumer protection line: (800) 727-6432
Fax: (402) 471-3297
E-mail: emrich@ago.state.ne.us

NEVADA

Greater Nevada Fair Housing Council
Address: 430 Jeanell Dr., Suite 2, Carson City, NV 89701
Phone: (702) 883-0888
Fax: (702) 883-5877

Nevada Attorney General's Office
Resources for renters.
Address: 100 N. Carson St., Carson City, NV 89701-4717
E-mail: aginfo@govmail.state.nv.us
Web site: http://www.state.nv.us/ag/

NEW HAMPSHIRE

New Hampshire Consumer Protection Bureau
Address: 33 Capitol St., Concord, NH 03301-6397
Phone: (603) 271-3641

New Hampshire Legal Advice and Referral Center
The site contains the texts of several useful pamphlets about tenants'
rights in New Hampshire.
Address: P.O. Box 4147, Concord, NH 03302-4147
Phone: (800) 639-5290 (603) 224-3333
Fax: (603) 224-6067
Web site: http://www.mv.com/ipusers/larc/

New Hampshire Revised Statutes
Searchable database of New Hampshire laws.
Web site: http://199.92.250.14/rsa/

Renting, Security Deposits, and Evictions in New Hampshire
Brochure prepared by the New Hampshire Consumer Protection Bureau.
Web site: http://www.state.nh.us/nhdoj/Consumer/rse.html

NEW JERSEY

Fair Housing Council of Northern New Jersey
Address: 131 Main St., Hackensack, NJ 07601
Phone: (201) 489-3552 (201) 489-4692
Fax: (201) 489-8472
E-mail: fhcnnj@bellatlantic.net
Web site: http://www.fairhousing.com/fhcnnj/

Fair Housing Council of Southern New Jersey
Address: 44 Cooper St., Woodbury, NJ 07601
Phone: (609) 848-7050 or (888) 537-8688
Fax: (609) 848-6644

Housing Coalition of Central Jersey
Address: 78 New St., Suite 3, New Brunswick, NJ 08901-2502
Phone: (908) 249-9700
Fax: (908) 249-4121

New Jersey Tenants Organization
Address: 389 Main St., Hackensack, NJ 07601
Phone: (201) 342-3775
Fax: (201) 342-3776
E-mail: NJTenants@injersey.com

NEW MEXICO

Landlord/Tenant Hot Line (New Mexico Public Interest Education Fund)
Provides information and referrals to tenants and landlords. They also provide organizational support and technical assistance to tenant organizations. Services are free to the public, and all materials are free with proof of low income.
Address: 115B Harvard SE, Albuquerque, NM 87106-3520
Phone: (505) 256-9442
Fax: (505) 256-1633

New Mexico Attorney General's Office, Consumer Protection Division
Landlord/tenant brochures (and other brochures) are available by mail. You can order them through http://www.ago.state.nm.us/publications/index.html.
Address: P.O. Drawer 1508, Bataan Memorial Building, Santa Fe, NM 87504
Statewide: (800) 678-1508
Santa Fe: (505) 827-6060
Recorded landlord/tenant information: (800) 300-2020 ext. 7726
Fax: (505) 827-6685
Web site: http://www.ago.state.nm.us/CPROTECT/index.html

Santa Fe Landlord/Tenant Hot Line
Address: 664 Alta Vista, Santa Fe, NM 87505
Phone: (505) 983-8447 or (800) 348-9370

NEW YORK

Greater Syracuse Tenant Network
The network was founded by low-income tenants, primarily in government-assisted housing, to advocate for improved housing conditions and affordable housing. It serves tenants in upstate New York.

Address: P.O. Box 6908, Syracuse, NY
Phone: (313) 475-8092
Fax: (315) 475-8274
E-mail: sharsher@aol.com

Mt. Vernon United Tenants
Address: 40 S. 4th Ave., Mt. Vernon, NY 10550-3105

New York Tenant Exchange
E-mail: tenant@tenant.net
Web site: http://www.nytenant.net/

Tenants Union of the West Side
Address: 200 W. 72nd St., Room 63, New York, NY 10023
Phone: (212) 595-1274

United Tenants of Albany
Address: 33 Clinton Ave., Albany, NY 12207
Phone: (518) 436-8997
Fax: (518) 436-0320

NORTH CAROLINA

Office of the Attorney General Consumer Protection
Address: P.O. Box 629, Raleigh, NC 27602-0629
Phone: (919) 716-6000
Fax: (919) 716-6050
E-mail: agjus@mail.jus.state.nc.us
Web site: http://www.jus.state.nc.us/cpframe.htm

Charlotte Organizing Project
Grassroots community organizers. Particular issues are tenants' rights, housing code enforcement, prevention of childhood lead poisoning, and preservation of Section 8 housing.
Address: 1515 Elizabeth Ave., Suite 200, Charlotte, NC 28204-2508
Phone: (704) 372-0675
Fax: (704) 332-0445
E-mail: chopc@bellsouth.net

North Carolina Fair Housing Center
Investigates alleged violations of fair housing statutes; provides assistance to people pursuing legal rights; promotes community involvement in fair housing issues; and performs research and policy development in the area of fair housing.
Address: 101 Saint Mary's St., Raleigh, NC 27604
Phone: (919) 856-2166
Fax: (919) 823-9235
E-mail: sadams7943@aol.com
Web site: http://www.fairhousing.com/ncfhc/

North Carolina Low-Income Housing Coalition
Address: 3901 Barrett Dr., Suite 200, Raleigh, NC 27609-6611
Phone: (919) 881-0707

NORTH DAKOTA

North Dakota Attorney General's Office
They have a downloadable brochure in PDF format.
Address: 600 E. Boulevard Ave., Bismarck, ND 58505-0040
Phone: (701) 328-2210
TTY: (701) 328-3409
Fax: (701) 328-2226
Web site: http://expedition.bismarck.ag.state.nd.us/ndag/

North Dakota Fair Housing Council
Works to eradicate housing discrimination through public education
and assistance to people experiencing housing discrimination.
Address: 533 Airport Rd., Bismarck, ND 58504
Phone: (701) 221-2530
TTY: (800) 927-9275
Fax: (701) 221.9597
Web site: http://www.fairhousing.com/ndfhc/

North Dakota Renters Hot Line
Phone: (701) 232-7368 or (800) 726-7960

OHIO

Cleveland Tenants Organization
Address: 2530 Superior Ave., Cleveland, OH 44115
Phone: (216) 621-0540 or (800) 450-0096
E-mail: HN7096@Handsnet.org
Web site: http://little.nhlink.net/nhlink/housing/cto/

Ohio Fair Housing Contact Service
Focuses on ending discrimination in housing; also counsels tenants and
landlords on their rights and responsibilities.
Address: 333 S. Main St., Suite 300B, Akron, OH 44308
Phone: (330) 376-6191
E-mail: ohiofhcs@aol.com
Web site: http://fhcs.fairhousing.com/

Ohio Landlord-Tenant Laws (Title 53 Section 5321)
Web site: http://orc.avv.com/title-53/sec-5321/whole.htm

OhioLandlordTenant.com
Notes about landlord-tenant law from the law offices of Andrew J. Ruzicho.
E-mail: lruzicho@columbus.rr.com
Web site: http://www.ohiolandlordtenant.com/

Toledo Fair Housing Center
Works to ensure that all who seek housing have an equal opportunity to
rent, purchase, finance, or insure the property they choose.
Address: 2116 Madison Ave., Toledo, OH 43624
Phone: (419) 243-6163 1-800-248-2840
Fax: (419) 243-3536
E-mail: fhctr@aol.com
Web site: http://www.toledofhc.org/

OKLAHOMA

Oklahoma Renter's Information
Provided and maintained by the Oklahoma State University Off-
Campus Student Association.
Web site: http://www.okstate.edu/osu_orgs/ocsa/noinfo.html

OREGON

Community Alliance of Tenants
Provides tenant counseling, organizing, and renters' rights forums.
Address: 2710 N.E. 14th St., Portland, OR 97212
Phone: (503) 460-9702
Fax: (503) 288-8416
E-mail: cat@aracnet.com

Fair Housing Council of Oregon
Address: 310 S.W. 4th Ave., Suite 430, Portland, OR 97204-2345

Phone: (503) 223-8295
TTY: (800) 424-3247
E-mail: fairhsor@teleport.com
Web site: http://www.fhco.org/

Landlord-Tenant Law in Oregon
Prepared by Oregon Legal Services as part of its Community Education
Series.
Web   site:
http://www.efn.org/~fairhous/eng/legalres/oregon/orlltleng.html

Manufactured Home Owners of Oregon, Inc./OSTA
Address: 3791-B River Rd. N, Keizer, OR 97303
Phone: (503) 393-7737(800) 423-9371
Fax: (503) 648-2261
Web site: http://www.mhoo-osta.com/

Southern Oregon Fair Housing Project
A service of the Southern Oregon Community Housing Resource
Board.
E-mail: fairhous@efn.org
Web site: http://www.efn.org/~fairhous/

Tel-Law Landlord/Tenant Information
A collection of recorded legal information messages prepared by the
Oregon State Bar.
Phone: (503) 620-3000
In-state toll free: (800) 452-4776
Web site: http://www.osbar.org/Public/AboutOregonLaw/TelLaw/home.html

PENNSYLVANIA

Harrisburg Fair Housing Council
Address: 1228 Bailey St., Harrisburg, PA 17103-2241
Phone: (717) 238-9540

Lehigh Valley Legal Services
Offers free legal services to low-income people in Lehigh and Northampton Counties. They staff a telephone hot line offering advice on housing and other issues.
Address: 65 E. Elizabeth Ave., Suite 903, Bethlehem, PA 18018-6506
Phone: (610) 317-8757
Fax: (610) 317-8778
E-mail: lvls@itw.com
Web site: http://www.lehighlegal.org/

Tenants' Action Group of Philadelphia (TAG)
Provides counseling, organizing, advocacy, and emergency grants.
Address: 21 S. 12th St., Floor 12, Philadelphia, PA 19107-3610
Phone: (215) 575-0700
Fax: (215) 575-0718
E-mail: TAGTRAC@critpath.org
Web site: http://www.womensway.org/agencies/tag.html

RHODE ISLAND

Rhode Island Attorney General's Office
There are many branch offices (see http://www.riag.state.ri.us/tour/).
Address: 150 S. Main St., Providence, RI 02903
Phone: (401) 274-4400
Fax: (401) 222-1331
Web site: http://www.riag.state.ri.us/

Rhode Island Landlord-Tenant Handbook
Produced by the Rhode Island Department of Administration
Statewide Planning Program.
Web site: http://www.lori.state.ri.us/landlord/

Rhode Island Residential Landlord and Tenant Act
Web site: http://www.rilin.state.ri.us/Statutes/TITLE34/34-18/INDEX.HTM

SOUTH CAROLINA

South Carolina Attorney General's Office
Address: Rembert Dennis Building, 1000 Assembly St., Room 501,
Columbia, SC 29211
Phone: (803) 734-3970 or (803) 734-4399
E-mail: info@scattorneygeneral.org
Web site: http://www.scattorneygeneral.org/

South Carolina Bar Association
Their "Lawline" contains answers to frequently asked legal questions,
including questions about landlords, tenants, and leases. Free legal help
is also available through a program called "Ask-A-Lawyer" and through
free legal clinics.
Address: 950 Taylor St., Columbia, SC 29202
Main office: (803) 799-6653
Ask-A-Lawyer: (888) 321-3644
Free legal clinics: (803) 799-6653 x 158
Fax: (803) 799-4118
E-mail: scbar-info@scbar.org
Web site: http://www.scbar.org/

SOUTH DAKOTA

South Dakota Office of the Attorney General, Division of Consumer Protection
Address: 500 E. Capitol Ave., Pierre, SD 57501
Phone: (605) 773-4400
In-state toll free: (800) 300-1986
E-mail: help@atg.state.sd.us
Web site: http://www.state.sd.us/state/executive/attorney/consumer/index.html

TENNESSEE

Knoxville Legal Aid Society
Serves community groups and low-income people in Knox, Blount, Loudon, and Sevier Counties.
Address: 502 S. Gay St. Suite 404, Knoxville, TN 37902
Phone: (423) 637-0484
Web site: http://www.korrnet.org/klas/

Nashville Bar Association
Provides a free "Dial-a-Lawyer" service on a regular basis.
Address: 221 4th Ave. N, Suite 400, Nashville, TN 37219-2100
Phone: (615) 242-9272
Fax: (615) 255-3026
Web site: http://www.nashbar.org/

Tennessee Division of Consumer Affairs
Provides consumer brochures, including some on tenants' rights; also has a short list of frequently asked questions about landlord-tenant affairs.
Address: 500 James Robertson Parkway, 5th Floor, Nashville, TN 37243-0600
Phone: (615) 741-4737

In-state toll free: (800) 342-8385
E-mail: dca@mail.state.tn.us
Web site: http://www.state.tn.us/consumer/

Tennessee Fair Housing Council
Address: 19 Thompson Lane, Suite 324, Nashville, TN 37206
Phone: (615) 383-6155 or (800) 254-2166
E-mail: house@fairhousing.com

TEXAS

Attorney General of Texas, Office of Consumer Protection
Landlord/tenant information from the attorney general's office is
available in PDF format at
http://www.oag.state.tx.us/AG_Publications/pdfs/tenant_rights.pdf.
Address: P.O. Box 12548, Austin, TX 78711-2548
Phone: (512) 463-2070
Web site: http://www.oag.state.tx.us/consumer/consumer.htm

Austin Tenants' Council
Address: 1619 E. Cesar Chavez, Austin, TX 78702
Phone: (512) 474-1961
Web site: http://www.housing-rights.org/

Dallas Tenants Association
Address: 3108 Live Oak St., Dallas, TX 75204
Phone: (214) 828-4244
Web site: http://www.housingcrisiscenter.org/dallas_tenants_association.html

Legal Aid of Central Texas
Phone: (512) 476-7244

Texas Low-Income Housing Information Service (TxLIHIS)
Produces the excellent *Texas Tenant Advisor*.
Address: 508 Powell St., Austin, TX 78703-5122
Phone: (512) 477-8910
Web site: http://www.texashousing.org/

Texas Tenants Union
Free weekly workshops on tenants' rights; organizing assistance at the
apartment-complex level; written information; counseling; training;
referral services.
Address: 5405 E. Grand Ave., Dallas, TX 75223
Phone: (214) 823-2733

The University of Texas Student Attorney
University of Texas students only.
Phone: (512) 471-7796
E-mail: raymonds@mail.utexas.edu

UTAH

Utah Attorney General's Office
Address: 236 State Capitol Building, Salt Lake City, UT 84114
Phone: (801) 538-9600
Fax: (801) 538-1121
Web site: http://www.attygen.state.ut.us/

Utah Renter's Handbook
Web site: http://www.union.utah.edu/rentbook.htm

Utah State Bar
Sponsors a free legal advice program in Salt Lake City called "Tuesday
Night Bar." For more information, see http://www.utahbar.org/

public/progs_serv/tuesday/tuesday.html, or call the bar at the number below.
Address: 645 S. 200 E, Salt Lake City, UT 84111
Phone: (801) 531-9077
Web site: http://www.utahbar.org/

VERMONT

Statewide tenants' rights organization providing information and referrals. Sponsors frequent tenants' rights workshops free of charge. Provides advice to tenants over the phone and in person concerning their rights as renters. Publishes the *Renting in Vermont Landlord-Tenant Handbook.*
Address: 191 North St., Burlington, VT 05401
Phone: (802) 864-0099 or (800) 287-7971
Web site: http://homepages.together.net/~tedvti/

VIRGINIA

City of Alexandria Office of Housing
Main office: 838-4990
Landlord-tenant relations division: 838-4545
Web site: http://ci.alexandria.va.us/city/kyc/kyc04.html

Housing Opportunities Made Equal (HOME)
Provides tenant counseling, discrimination testing, down-payment assistance, and other services.
Address: 1218 W. Cary St., Richmond, VA 23220
Phone: (804) 354-0641
Fax: (804) 354-0690
Web site: http://www.phonehome.org/

Off-Campus Housing Office, Virginia Commonwealth University
Take a virtual tour designed for first-time renters, check out local rental listings, or print out some useful forms.
Address: Richmond, VA 23230
Phone: (804) 828-6492
Web site: http://www.vcu.edu/safweb/commons/infooch.html

The Arlington County Housing Information Center
Phone: (703) 228-3765

Virginia Fair Housing Office
Address: 3600 W. Broad St., 5th Floor, Room 554, Richmond, VA 23230
Phone: (804) 367-8530
Fax: (804) 367-0047
E-mail: fairhousing@dpor.state.va.us
Web site: http://www.state.va.us/dpor/fairhs01.htm

WASHINGTON

The Tenants Union
Helps tenants understand their legal rights, advocates for better laws for tenants, and assists tenants who wish to form tenant associations in their building. Also produces an action-alert mailing list providing news and information about tenants, rights in Seattle and the entire state.
Address: 3902 S. Ferdinand St., Seattle, WA 98118
Phone: (206) 723-0500
TTY: (206) 723-0523
Fax: (206) 725-3527
Web site: http://www.tenantsunion.org

The Tenants Union's Referrals List
Links and contact information for various tenant-related organizations and services in Washington.
Web site: http://www.tenantsunion.org/referrals.html

WEST VIRGINIA

West Virginia Attorney General's Office
Address: 1900 Kanawha Blvd., Room 26E, Charleston, WV 25305-9924
Phone: (304) 558-2021
E-mail: consumer@wvnet.edu
Web site: http://www.state.wv.us/wvag/

WISCONSIN

Tenant Resource Center
Address: 122 State St., Suite 310, Madison, WI 53703
Business/main office: (608) 257-0143
Housing counseling: (608) 257-0006
Housing help desk: (608) 242-7406
Mediation: (608) 257-2799
Fax: (608) 286-0804

Tenants' Rights and Responsibilities in Wisconsin
Provided by the West Bend Police Department.
Web site: http://www.ci.west-bend.wi.us/cops/tenants.htm

Wisconsin Legislative Information
Search the statutes for information about landlords and tenants, or use this index to Wisconsin landlord-tenant statutes.
Web site: http://folio.legis.state.wi.us/

WYOMING

Wyoming Attorney General's Office
Address: 123 Capitol Building, Cheyenne, WY 82002
Phone: (307) 777-7841
E-mail: consumer@wvnet.edu
Web site: http://www.state.wy.us/~ag/

APPENDIX K

Fair Housing Information

THE FAIR HOUSING ACT

The Fair Housing Act prohibits discrimination in housing based of any of the following:
- Race or color
- National origin
- Religion
- Sex
- Familial status (including children under the age of eighteen living with parents or legal custodians; pregnant women and people securing custody of children under eighteen years old)
- Handicap

What Housing Is Covered?

The Fair Housing Act covers most housing. In some circumstances, the act exempts owner-occupied buildings with no more than four units, single-family housing sold or rented without the use of a broker, and housing operated by organizations and private clubs that limit occupancy to members.

What Is Prohibited?

In the sale and rental of housing: No one may take any of the following actions based on race, color, national origin, religion, sex, familial status, or handicap:

- Refuse to rent or sell housing
- Refuse to negotiate for housing
- Make housing unavailable
- Deny a dwelling
- Set different terms, conditions, or privileges for sale or rental of a dwelling
- Provide different housing services or facilities
- Falsely deny that housing is available for inspection, sale, or rental
- For profit, persuade owners to sell or rent (blockbusting)
- Deny anyone access to or membership in a facility or service (such as a multiple-listing service) related to the sale or rental of housing

In addition: It is illegal for anyone to do any of the following:

- Threaten, coerce, intimidate, or interfere with anyone exercising a fair housing right or assisting others who exercise that right
- Advertise or make any statement that indicates a limitation or preference based on race, color, national origin, religion, sex, familial status, or handicap. This prohibition against discriminatory advertising applies to single-family and owner-occupied housing that is otherwise exempt from the Fair Housing Act.

Significant Recent Changes

1. In addition to expanding the number of protected classes and creating new enforcement procedures, the 1988 amendments to the Fair Housing Act also created an exemption to the provisions baring discrimination on the basis of familial status for those housing developments that qualified as housing for persons age fifty-five or older.

The Housing for Older Persons Act (HOPA) of 1995 made several changes to the fifty-five-and-older exemption. First, it eliminated the requirement that fifty-five-and-older housing had "significant facilities and services" designed for the elderly. Second, HOPA established "good faith reliance" immunity from damages for persons who, in good faith, believed that the fifty-five-and-older exemption applied to a particular property, if they did not actually know that the property was not eligible for the exemption and if the property had formally stated in writing that it qualified for the exemption.

HOPA retains the requirement that housing must have one person who is fifty-five years of age or older living in at least 80 percent of its occupied units. It also still requires that housing publish and follow policies and procedures that demonstrate intent to be housing for persons fifty-five and older (rather than housing for adults or for singles, for example).

An exempt property will not violate the Fair Housing Act if it excludes families with children, but it does not have to do so. Of course, the property must meet the act's requirements that at least 80 percent of its occupied units have at least one occupant who is fifty-five or older, and that it publish and follow policies and procedures that demonstrate an intent to be fifty-five-and-older housing.

Housing and Urban Development (HUD) has prepared proposed regulations as required by Congress, and they were published for public comment on January 14, 1997. Once final regulations have officially been adopted, HUD will remove regulations outdated as a result of the changed law.

2. Changes were made to enhance law enforcement, including amendments to criminal penalties in Section 901 of the Civil Rights Act of 1968 for violations of the Fair Housing Act in Title VIII. See Section 320103(e) of the Violent Crime Control and Law Enforcement Act of 1994. P.L. 103-322 (9/13/94).

3. Changes were made to provide incentives for self-testing by lenders for discrimination under the Fair Housing Act and the Equal Credit Opportunity Act. See Title II, Subtitle D of the Omnibus Consolidated Appropriations Act, 1997, P.L. 104-208 (9/30/96). Legal Authority: Fair Housing Act, 42 U.S.C. 3601, et seq; 24 CFR Parts 100,103, and 104. Program Status: Fair Housing Enforcement (Title VIII), which excludes grant programs, is covered by Salaries and Expense Account appropriations.

ADDITIONAL PROTECTION IF YOU HAVE A DISABILITY

If you or someone associated with you

- have a physical or mental disability (including hearing, mobility, and visual impairments, chronic alcoholism, chronic mental illness, AIDS, AIDS Related Complex, and mental retardation) that substantially limits one or more major life activities,
- have a record of such a disability, or
- are regarded as having such a disability,

your landlord cannot

- refuse to let you make reasonable modifications to your dwelling or common-use areas, at your expense, if necessary for the handicapped person to use the housing. (Where reasonable, the landlord may permit changes only if you agree to restore the property to its original condition when you move.)
- refuse to make reasonable accommodations in rules, policies, practices, or services if necessary for the handicapped person to use the housing.

Example: A building with a "no pets" policy must allow a visually impaired tenant to keep a guide dog.

Example: An apartment complex that offers tenants ample, unassigned parking must honor a request from a mobility impaired tenant for a reserved space near his or her apartment if necessary to assure access to his or her apartment.

However, housing need not be made available to a person who is a direct threat to the health or safety of others or who currently uses illegal drugs.

REQUIREMENTS FOR NEW BUILDINGS

In buildings that were ready for first occupancy after March 13, 1991, and have an elevator and four or more units, the following requirements apply:

- Public and common areas must be accessible to persons with disabilities.
- Doors and hallways must be wide enough for wheelchairs.
- All units must have the following:
- an accessible route into and through the unit

- accessible light switches, electrical outlets, thermostats, and other environmental controls
- reinforced bathroom walls to allow later installation of grab bars
- kitchens and bathrooms that can be used by people in wheelchairs

If a building with four or more units has no elevator and was ready for first occupancy after March 13, 1991, these standards apply to ground-floor units. These requirements for new buildings do not replace any more stringent standards in Title II of the Americans with Disabilities Act (ADA) of 1990, which prohibits discrimination against persons with disabilities in all services, programs, and activities made available by state and local governments. The Department of Justice (DOJ) has coordination authority for the ADA in accordance with Executive Order 11250.

The DOJ regulations cover all state and local governments and extend the prohibition of discrimination in federally assisted programs established by Section 504 of the Rehabilitation Act of 1973 to all activities of state and local governments, including those that do not receive federal financial assistance.

Housing and Urban Development (HUD) is the designated agency for all programs, services, and regulatory activities relating to state and local public housing, and housing assistance and referrals. In addition, HUD has jurisdiction over a state or local government activity when HUD has jurisdiction under Section 504 of the Rehabilitation Act of 1973. Legal Authority: Americans with Disabilities Act of 1990 42 USC 12131; DOJ regulation; 28 CFR Part 35.

APPENDIX L

ROOMMATE DON'TS

- Don't allow others to pick your roommates.
- Don't try to be a therapist or counselor; leave it to the professionals. You can, however, be a good listener.
- Don't talk about your roomie, or their personal problems, with outsiders.
- Don't steal your roommate's date.
- Don't assume you can live with someone based on his or her good looks or lack of them.
- Don't share razors, deodorants, toothbrushes, or other obviously personal items.
- Don't wear your roommate's clothes unless he or she says it's okay—even then, clean it after you wear it.
- Don't loan out your roommate's things.
- Don't plan an event, party, et cetera, in the unit until you clear it with your roommate.
- Don't loan money to your roommate; it's the best way to ruin a friendship.
- Don't buy something and expect your roomie to pay half the cost if you have not told him or her about the item or service prior to the purchase.

- Don't disappear from the unit for several days without telling your roomie where you are going and/or how you can be contacted.
- Don't assume your roommate likes rap, punk, ska, or heavy metal at all hours; use your headphones.
- Don't assume you have to do everything together just because you are roomies. You both need time and space away from each other.
- Don't assume your best friend from high school or work will be the best roommate.
- Don't invite friends over and ignore your roommate or leave him or her out of the conversation.
- Don't adopt a pet without letting your roommate know and getting his or her approval.
- Don't eat what you haven't paid for.
- Don't eat or drink the last of anything and leave the empty receptacle.
- Don't buy big-ticket items, such as a refrigerator, together—especially if the payments go beyond the lease.
- Don't get angry and sulk and then expect your roommate to know why you are upset.
- Don't borrow anything without asking.
- Don't assume that because you are from the same town, school, or church that you will get along.
- Don't assume that because you are of a different race, ethnic origin, religious background, or sexual orientation that you won't get along.
- Don't give out keys to the unit to other people.
- Don't change your values or beliefs to fit your roommate's needs.
- Don't let things or feelings build up to the point of explosion.
- Don't leave unpaid utility or phone bills.
- Don't move out without turning in your keys.
- Don't avoid paying your last month's rent based on the assumption that it can be taken out of your security deposit.

BIBLIOGRAPHY

- C. E. Rollins, 1994. 52 Ways to Get Along with Your College Roommate. Nashville, Tenn.: Thomas Nelson Publishers.
- Clifford Yorks, District Justice State College PA. Apartment Owners Managers meeting State College, PA Winter 1991.
- Jason Collington, "Renters Rights; Do You Know Yours?" The Daily O' Collegian on the Web, September 11, 1996 <www.ocolly.com> (18 May 2000).
- Landlord Rights and Responsibilities Centre Region Council of Governments Rental Housing Advisory Commission Spring 1993
- Larry Lick Sr., "Landlord-Tenant Rental Housing Law". Rental Housing On Line 3 February 2001 <http://www.cses.com/rental/ltlaw.htm#us.> (18 May 2000)
- Larry Lick Sr., "Rental Housing On Line Home" Page. 3 February 2001 <http://rhol.org/ rental/homepage.htm>. (18 May 2000)
- Mark DiCamillo Deposit Saver.Helping You Get In The Door Home Page, 2000 <http://www.depositsaver.com> (25 May 2000)
- Microsoft Network Neighborhood Finder. October 2000 <http://homeadvisor.msn. com/ns/neighborhoods/finder_dl.asp>(10 June 2000).
- Nancy O Andrews,. "Trends in the Supply of Affordable Housing." Meeting America's Housing Needs (MAHN): A Habitat II Follow-up Project" April 1998 <http://www.nlihc.org/mahn/ supply.htm.> (19 May 2000),

- Off Campus Student Association Oklahoma State University Renters Advisory Council. 9 October 1997 <http://www.okstate.edu/osu_orgs/ocsa/noinfo.html> (15 June 2000)
- Paula Shutkever, Student UK Home Page "Sharing a Flat 1998 <http://www. studentuk.com>.(24, May 2000).
- Rental Housing On Line The Tenant Resource Directory Information Resource for Renters throughout the United States. <http://directory.tenantsunion.org/>.
- Richard Sanders, Poor Richard Almanack 1732 Philadelphia Printed B. Franklin
- Tenant Landlord Handbook. 1994-2001<http://tenant.net/ Other_Areas /Penn/ harris/pa-toc.html>. (24 May 2000)
- "U.S. Department of Housing and Urban Development Section VIII Fair Housing and Equal 5 December 2000 Opportunity <http://www.hud.gov/sec8.html#a.> (12 January 2001).

INDEX